Nicholas Vincent is a professor of Medieval History at the University of East Anglia, specializing in twelfth- and thirteenth-century history, with a particular current focus on the Magna Carta. He is a Fellow of the British Academy.

NICHOLAS VINCENT

John
An Evil King?

PENGUIN BOOKS

PENGUIN BOOKS

UK | USA | Canada | Ireland | Australia
India | New Zealand | South Africa

Penguin Books is part of the Penguin Random House group of companies
whose addresses can be found at global.penguinrandomhouse.com

First published by Allen Lane 2020
Published in Penguin Books 2022
001

Copyright © Nicholas Vincent, 2020

The moral right of the author has been asserted

Typeset by Jouve (UK), Milton Keynes
Printed and bound in Great Britain by Clays Ltd, Elcograf S.p.A.

The authorized representative in the EEA is Penguin Random House Ireland,
Morrison Chambers, 32 Nassau Street, Dublin D02 YH68

ISBN: 978-0-141-99938-8

www.greenpenguin.co.uk

Penguin Random House is committed to a
sustainable future for our business, our readers
and our planet. This book is made from Forest
Stewardship Council® certified paper.

Contents

JOHN

For Daisy Aoife Elizabeth,
against whom King John would most definitely
not have prevailed

Introduction
King John and the Historians

King John ruled England for seventeen and a half years, from 1199 to 1216. For most of that time he enjoyed if not popularity, then great wealth and power. Yet to posterity his entire reign has come to be embodied in a single image. Furious, outmanoeuvred, crippled with vice, the king sits at Runnymede putting his royal seal on, or more often (anachronistically) signing, Magna Carta. No matter whether we approach this event as reactionaries wishing that he would assert himself, as conservatives delighted by the restoration of constitutional 'rights', or as radicals longing for liberty and revolution, Runnymede changes everything in our perception of King John. Seventeen years of history are reduced to a picnic on the banks of the Thames. John is exposed as villainous and pathetic. The people triumph. Tyranny is righted. John's foreign vices yield to English virtue.

Of course, things were not really so. Like all great moments in history, John's encounter at Runnymede warps our perception of the before and after. Since the ending is known, his becomes a reign written backwards, a series of events leading towards the signing of Magna Carta: a search for explanations of what 'went wrong'. Several of

John's modern biographers make this their central task. Two of the most recent specifically incorporate the words 'the road to Magna Carta' within their book titles. Sidney Painter, author of the most detailed and to date the best modern account of the period, explicitly framed his *Reign of King John* as an attempt 'to delineate fully the background and immediate consequences of the issuance of Magna Carta'.[1]

Not only this, but John's climactic humiliation was itself mythologized and distorted. What happened at Runnymede has echoed down the ages as a towering achievement. 'What say the reeds at Runnymede?' as Kipling's poem questions, before providing the answer: 'Your rights were won at Runnymede!'[2] Across Victorian England, carved, moulded or painted on town halls and other civic buildings from Rochdale to Westminster, the anachronistic image of John signing Magna Carta became iconic: a foundational moment for all English liberties and laws. Yet the charter issued at Runnymede was a failure, not a success. Intended to bring peace, it instead provoked war. Accepted in June 1215, it survived as law for less than twelve weeks. By early September 1215, it had been repudiated by king, Pope and barons. As a result, not only is the history of John's reign written backwards, but upside down. The king's greatest humiliation becomes his crowning achievement, the nucleus around which all else coheres.

In reality, John's reign involved rather more than a summer's morning at Runnymede. Two scenes in particular found their way into all pre-Victorian popular histories. Neither was exactly flattering to the king. First, there was the murder of his young nephew, Arthur of Brittany. From this act of infamy could be traced many consequences, not least the rebellion of John's French subjects and the loss of the continental estates that he and his ancestors had controlled since the Norman Conquest of 1066. Then there was the encounter outside Dover in 1213, in which, to stave off the threat of French invasion, the king placed England under papal lordship. From the 1520s onwards, Englishmen knew no greater bogeyman than the Pope, not even the King of France. John's surrender to the papacy was therefore interpreted as both sinister and heroic: a defensive ruse, intended to outwit those twin towers of evil, Paris and Rome.

The outcome here was a portrayal of John in tragi-heroic terms. He appears thus in fictional accounts – such as the play *King Johan* written by John Bale in 1538, and Shakespeare's *King John* from the mid 1590s – as a great reformer of the law, betrayed by monks, cardinals and other Catholic conspirators. In the process, the events of 1215 were brushed away. Neither Bale nor Shakespeare referred to Runnymede or Magna Carta, although both playwrights dramatized the baronial rebellion and the alliance between Church and rebels as proof of the king's victimization by a seditious and disloyal French baronage duped by Rome. This was the image of John's reign promulgated in *Foxe's Book of Martyrs*, published in 1563: after the Bible, the Protestant Reformation's greatest best-seller.

A change in attitudes came only slowly. It began in the 1620s with attempts to present John's reign as a model for what was wrong with the Stuart kings. Just as John had

been restrained by Magna Carta, so lawyers and parliamen-
tarians argued, James I and Charles I should be taught
respect for the majestic antiquity of English law. John himself became the archetypal tyrant. It was thus that he appears
in the 1760s, in David Hume's *History of England*. Hume
convicts John of a catalogue of crimes: 'cowardice, in-
activity, folly, levity, licentiousness, ingratitude, treachery,
tyranny, and cruelty', and much more besides. Far from
defending his people against Rome or France, Hume's John
lost 'dominions . . . more extensive than have, ever since his
time, been ruled by any English monarch'.[3] In the age of
American independence, John was portrayed as a greater
failure even than King George III, the king blamed for the
loss of Britain's American colonies.

For the full flowering of the black legend of King John
we must none the less wait until 1819 and the publication
of Sir Walter Scott's *Ivanhoe*. Here at last we find John
portrayed, even before his succession as king, as coward,
lecher and would-be tyrant: the very model of all that was
unmanly, unnatural and un-British. Above all, we find
John as a French speaker, surrounded by a coterie of bullying and untrustworthy French sycophants. 'Prince John,' so
Scott reports, 'hated and contemned the few Saxon families
of consequence which subsisted in England, and omitted no
opportunity of mortifying and affronting them.'[4]

This view of England, as late as 1200 still bitterly divided between French aristocratic landlords and a tenantry
composed of the dispossessed and resentful Saxon victims
of 1066, was almost entirely Scott's invention. It was a
fiction that none the less enjoyed immense appeal in the

nineteenth century, not least – and ironically enough – in France where it was popularized through Augustin Thierry's supposedly 'scientific' (in reality heavily romanticized) *History of the Conquest of England by the Normans*, published six years after *Ivanhoe*. Throw in the even more romanticized legends of Robin Hood – themselves known from versions first circulating in the fifteenth century, heavily embellished from the eighteenth century onwards – and we reach what in due course became the Hollywood view of King John. Here in the many cinematic versions of Robin Hood or *Ivanhoe* we find the king impersonated, and in the process travestied, by Claude Rains (*Robin Hood*, 1938), Ian Holm (*Robin and Marian*, 1976) or Peter Ustinov (as the cartoon villain of Disney's *Robin Hood*, 1973). Here at last, as the result of Victorian replumbing and rewiring, we encounter the version of King John who, in the words of William Stubbs, greatest of all Victorian medievalists, was 'the very worst of all our kings . . . polluted with every crime that could disgrace a man'.[5]

Where does all this history of history lead us? How, after all these 'spoilers', can we approach a king whom contemporaries knew to be a failure, and whom subsequent historians have portrayed not as a human being but as the very embodiment of evil? John has gone down in history not as a personality but as an explanation for constitutional developments that, in his own lifetime, would have seemed both fleeting and, to many, entirely obnoxious. Like Herod, Nero or any other notorious tyrant, John has many critics, a few defenders, but fewer impartial biographers.

We have no physical description of King John. His height,

to judge from his skeleton and tomb effigy, was about five feet six inches: considerable in twelfth-century terms, but less than that of his father or elder brother.[6] The chroniclers who report his evil deeds for the most part wrote with hindsight rather than in John's own lifetime. It used to be asserted that those who actually met him, such as Roger of Howden whose chronicle ends in 1201, wrote of John favourably or at least neutrally, without the loathing shown by later writers. In reality, it is now agreed, Howden reported little that was favourable to John, and that only at the very beginning of the reign. Thereafter even Howden came to see quite how disastrously things were developing.

In what follows we shall first trace John's deeds, and only then turn to the king's personality. Such a division can never be entirely clear-cut, least of all in the case of a medieval king such as John who did not merely reign but rule. The king was both warlord and symbolic father of his people, a dual identity displayed most clearly on the two-sided wax seal with which John authenticated his letters and laws. On one side of this seal, he is shown riding into battle with sword and shield, on the other enthroned in majesty dispensing justice. The quality of the workmanship of John's seal is itself remarkable. This was a king who in all things craved the very finest. The warrior side shows him carrying a shield on which the royal coat of arms, the three leopards of England, is for the first time clearly displayed. His sword is grooved, or 'fullered', in accordance with the latest military fashion. The legend or inscription to the seal reveals the king's identity. John is 'by God's grace King of England, Lord of Ireland, Duke of

Normandy and Aquitaine and Count of Anjou'. Here there is yet another innovation, for the first time introducing Ireland to the royal style.

But in both of the functions proclaimed on his seal, as warlord and dispenser of justice, John proved a failure. He proved no less a failure in governing the regions of England and France over which his seal proclaimed his authority. Only in his new lordship of Ireland was John to enjoy any degree of success, and even there, as we shall see, with disastrous consequences.

In an age in which victory in battle demonstrated God's approval, John lost the greatest of his wars, both in 1203 and 1214 fleeing from battle so that the French now occupied Normandy and all of what had previously been the Plantagenet lands, as far south as the River Loire. The 1215 rebellion in England was a direct consequence of John's French defeat the year before. In France, Ireland and throughout the British Isles, people came to believe him not merely incompetent or unlucky but actively responsible for acts of violence and cruelty that, if proved, would have branded him criminally wicked. Assuming that John was a 'bad' man and his reign a 'failure', we find in the sources what we expect to find, not what John himself might have wished us to discover. Even so, the records of John's reign are more revealing than might be supposed. Besides the slings and arrows directed against him by medieval chroniclers, we have an extraordinary resource in the letters and financial accounts of the king's own administration, especially the chancery rolls, which will be covered in more detail below. These on occasion, fleetingly but vividly, allow us access to more private thoughts. There is sufficient psychological insight here for us to build a picture of causes as well as effects. It is with underlying causes that this account is chiefly concerned. The choice of particular events will itself impose a pattern, albeit in this instance a pattern that was as clear to John's contemporaries as it has remained to posterity. Sometimes, as in the case of King John, both a king's contemporaries and later historians can agree on certain underlying truths. John was a bad king. But was he bad because unlucky, or bad because he was inherently evil?

A Note on Money

The basic unit of currency at this time was the silver penny, with twelve pennies making up a shilling, and twenty shillings considered to weigh 'one pound' of silver (hence pennies, shillings and pounds). For accounting purposes, sums were sometimes expressed not in pounds but in in 'marks': a 'mark' being equivalent to two-thirds of a pound, or thirteen shillings and fourpence. The only actual coins in circulation, however, at least in theory, remained silver pennies, twelve to a shilling and two hundred and forty to a pound. To convert thirteenth-century prices into modern equivalents is a treacherous business. Some historians suggest a multiplier of a thousand to convert into modern values, so that £1 in John's reign would today be worth £1,000. However, there are vast disparities here between the relative values of particular goods and services. On a very rough calculation, the king's ordinary income approached £25,000 a year; that of a dozen or so of the very richest of his barons was in excess of £1,000. For a majority even of the elite an annual income of £100 would have qualified a baron as wealthy.

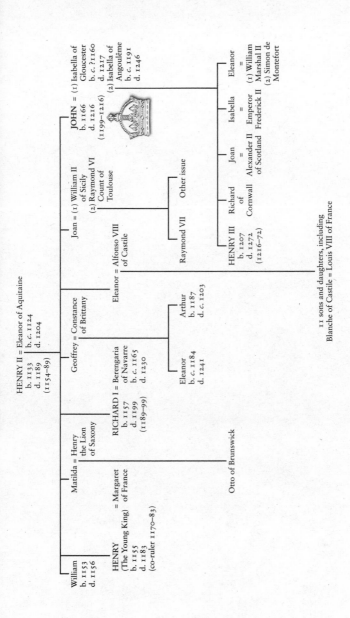

Britain and France in the time of King John

John

I
Childhood, Youth and Exile

John was never meant to be king. Born shortly after Christmas Day 1166, he was given a distinctly unroyal name, probably in honour of St John the Evangelist, whose feast day fell on 27 December. John's elder brothers had all been named after ruling ancestors, the eldest after previous Norman kings of England (William, Henry), Richard after a former duke of Normandy, and Geoffrey after John's paternal grandfather, who, as Count of Anjou, was the founder of the 'Angevin' dynasty from which John sprang. John, by contrast, was named after no king or duke or count, but after the disciple 'whom Jesus loved'.[1] He may well have been intended for a career in the Church: by this time, 'John' had been adopted as the name of no less than nineteen popes. Certainly, with three elder brothers – Henry, Richard and Geoffrey – all surviving into adulthood, there seemed no immediate prospect of John receiving land or dominion. Later tradition asserts that he was sent to be educated at Fontevraud on the Loire. A nunnery, served by male priests, lying on a cultural and political fault-line dividing northern France from the duchy of Aquitaine, Fontevraud had long attracted patronage from John's father and mother.

John's father, Henry II, was not the son of a king, but of Geoffrey Plantagenet, Count of Anjou, ruler of the cities of the Loire Valley. John's mother, Eleanor, was the elder daughter of Duke William X of Aquitaine, ruler of an even vaster estate that, in theory at least, stretched from the Loire south to the Pyrenees and from the Atlantic coast to the Massif Central. Duke William's inheritance, with its ducal palaces at Poitiers and Bordeaux, was a rich prize. It passed initially to Eleanor and her first husband, King Louis VII of France, and then, when her marriage to Louis was annulled in 1152, to her new husband, Henry of Anjou. Two years later, following the death of his rival and cousin King Stephen of England, Henry II succeeded to the English throne. With extraordinary speed and in the most improbable of circumstances, in 1154 John's father and mother became England's king and queen, as well as rulers of Normandy, the Loire Valley and the whole of Aquitaine as far south as the frontier with Spain.

From the moment of its birth, this Angevin empire was a magnificent yet fragile affair. The most extensive landed estate assembled by any French-speaking dynasty since the collapse of the empire of Charlemagne three hundred years before, it lacked any common language, administration or political culture. Eleanor, John's mother, came from a part of France where Occitan was spoken (employing the word *oc* rather than *oui* for the English 'yes'). By contrast, the French spoken by Henry II, learned on the Loire or in Normandy, would have been partially incomprehensible to his wife's family from the south, just as the French spoken in England was mocked at the court of the kings of France. As

an Angevin, from Anjou, Henry II was regarded as an outsider both in England and in Normandy, the only parts of
his empire placed under tight administrative control. Thanks
to its long tradition of tax-paying, England was crucial to
the empire's financial stability. Yet the English Channel rep-
resented a formidable barrier. From December to April it
was hazardous for shipping, and even in summer it remained
prone to storms and shipwreck. The Angevin claim to the
English throne, indeed, derived from the death without
male heirs of Henry II's maternal grandfather, King Henry
I, this lack of heirs itself a consequence of the drowning of
Henry I's only son, William, in the *White Ship* disaster of
1120. Like the Atlantic to later English empire-builders, the
Channel sundered empire from imperialists, with the *White
Ship* as its long-remembered *Titanic*.

Across the Channel, Angevin France was a far from uni-
fied affair. Normandy had two capitals (Rouen and Caen),
the Angevin lands further south at least three (Angers, Tours
and Le Mans). Beyond the Loire stretched Aquitaine which,
unaccustomed to northern government, fractured into a series of provinces with their own counts and viscounts, in
many cases openly contemptuous of rule from Poitiers or
Bordeaux, let alone of their new Angevin 'king'. The 'King
of the North', John's father was called in Aquitaine. In
Paris he was known as the 'King of London'.[2]

Throughout these great but scattered dominions, in
England as elsewhere, order could be maintained only by
ceaseless royal progresses that brought the itinerant king
into personal contact with regional noblemen otherwise
all too liable to revolt. No wonder that John, and his father

before him, acquired an awesome reputation for travel, moving daily from one residence to another, more or less permanently on horseback. Over time, the effect of these journeys was debilitating, both on a personal and a political level. By the end of his life, aged fifty-six, Henry II was so worn out by travel and poor circulation that he could barely stand on his own two, permanently swollen feet. John inherited this crippling infirmity. All of his brothers suffered early deaths: Henry 'the Young King' (so named as the son of King Henry II) aged twenty-eight, Geoffrey at twenty-seven, Richard at forty-one. Both Geoffrey and Richard were fatally injured on horseback. John himself was to die just short of his fiftieth birthday.

In political terms, too, this was an unstable family, its internecine quarrels and hatreds perceived as reflecting its rootlessness and lack of permanence. Contemporaries compared the Angevins to the wild huntsmen of legend and Welsh myth. They were also encouraged, not least by the Angevins themselves, to think of the royal family as diabolic. Both John's father and elder brother Richard boasted that they were descended from a she-devil, Mélusine, legendary ancestress of the counts of Anjou. Asked his opinion of the future Henry II, Saint Bernard of Clairvaux, the most holy man in Christendom, declared: 'From the Devil he came, and to the Devil he will surely go.'[3] This 'Devil's brood' toyed with cruelty as if it were a family heirloom. There was competition at court as to who could deliver the most off-colour remarks, the most humiliating put-downs. John's grandfather Geoffrey of Anjou, so it was rumoured, having ordered the castration of one of his bishops, forced the bishop to process through the streets of his cathedral city carrying his testicles in a jar before him. No matter that the story was probably invented: this was a family that rejoiced in the macabre. It was Geoffrey, too, who bequeathed another name to his descendants, from the sprig of yellow-flowered broom that he adopted as a badge: in French the *plant-de-genêt*, hence the 'Plantagenets', a name used as an alternative to their description as 'Angevins'.

At the Christmas feast of 1170, when John himself was approaching his fourth birthday, Angevin outrageousness was taken a step further and provoked notorious bloodshed. Tired of the endless cavilling of Thomas Becket, his Archbishop of Canterbury and former servant, John's father Henry spoke words in anger, and quite possibly drink, that even he later admitted should never have been spoken. Four knights took the king's words at face value, crossed from Normandy to England, and murdered Becket. The whole of Christendom condemned the killing; the Pope almost immediately declared Becket a saint. As with similar outrages down the ages, Becket's murder in some ways merely added to the sinister glamour of those who had commanded it. Certainly, Henry II kept his throne. A year after Becket's death, Henry crossed to Ireland intending to add yet another piece to his already complex territorial jigsaw.

Through all of this ran another theme. The Angevins had no permanent home. They also had no history as kings. Henry II's father was born as heir to a count, not a king. Henry's and hence John's claim to the English throne came through Henry's mother, Matilda, daughter of King

Henry I. Parvenus, sprung from nowhere, how could this family possibly rival the true kings of France? In Paris there dwelt a dynasty, the Capetians, claiming direct descent from the even more ancient lines of Carolingians and Merovingians, stretching all the way back to the time, seven centuries before, when Roman Gaul had first been conquered by the marauding Franks. In practical terms, these Capetian kings of France governed lands less extensive than those of the Angevin kings of England. Their lordship or 'demesne' was confined to the region between the rivers Somme, Marne, Yonne and Loire: a land-locked 'island', hence the 'Île-de-France' with Paris at its centre. In terms of charisma, however, the Capetians towered over all rivals. It was they who guarded the tombs and relics of their royal ancestors. They who, in association with the Pope, commanded crusades. They who had the right to be crowned and anointed with holy oil at Rheims. They who could lay claim to the mantle of Charlemagne.

Louis VII, King of France, had been married to Eleanor of Aquitaine, John's mother, from 1137 to 1152, before her divorce from Louis and her subsequent marriage to John's father. Paris depended upon the trade of the River Seine, flowing downstream through Normandy to Rouen and the sea. Conflict between Plantagenets and Capetians here was unavoidable. The Capetians could not allow a rival to seize the whole of western France or to encroach so close and so menacingly to Paris, their chief city. For a time, they were outwitted by John's father and mother. Louis VII was no military genius. As late as 1165, he lacked a son to succeed him. But with the coming of this heir, things changed. Philip

Augustus, Louis's son, born just over a year before John, was a cleverer man than his father. As we shall see, he was also to prove a far wiser man than his chief rival, King John.

We can trace the earliest Plantagenet anxieties here back to the 1170s. By this time, both John and Philip were still only six or seven years old. In February 1173, John was betrothed by his father to a daughter of the Count of Savoy, the region of northern Italy/south-eastern France straddling the Alpine passes. On the face of things, the deal was highly advantageous. Through marriage John, and hence his father, would acquire direct access to Italy. Turin would become an Angevin city. As part of a wider settlement, the whole of south-central France, from Toulouse via the Massif Central to the Alps, would be placed under Angevin protection, detached from the realm in theory dependent on the Capetian kings in Paris. To secure this deal, John was persuaded to turn down the even more glittering prospect of marriage to a daughter of the Byzantine emperor of Constantinople. John's Savoyard betrothal, however, provoked discontent within his own family.

His elder brothers, Henry, Richard and Geoffrey, objected to their father's interference with their own future prospects. Moreover, while the Count of Savoy offered much, he expected favours in return. What lands, he demanded to know, would Henry II bestow on John to match those in Savoy that John would acquire through marriage? In February 1173, Henry II promised three castles on the Loire, including the great fortress of Chinon: one of the most treasured possessions of John's eldest brother, Henry the Young King. This their father was now proposing to bestow on John. The offer spurred the young Henry into rebellion. Encouraged by their mother, John's brothers Richard and Geoffrey joined the revolt, placing themselves under the protection of Louis of France.

For Henry II, this was a potentially catastrophic scenario. Already tarnished by his involvement in Becket's murder, he was confronted by a great alliance that drew in not only his now estranged wife and his sons but the rulers of France, Flanders and Scotland. He seemed doomed to humiliation. Tensions held in check since his accession in 1154, not least among a powerful constituency of English barons whose wealth and castles the king had plundered, now exploded into civil war. The Earls of Leicester, Norfolk and Chester joined the revolt. Even the king's cousin, the Earl of Gloucester, was suspected of rebel sympathies. John himself was too young to play any direct part in this conflict. It was none the less one of the formative experiences of his childhood, directly provoked by his own promotion in Savoy.

Having goaded his sons and critics into an open display of rebellion, Henry picked off each of the chief conspirators in turn. Queen Eleanor was taken captive and for the next fifteen years consigned to house arrest in southern England. The armies assembled by the Earls of Leicester and Norfolk and the Count of Flanders were defeated in battle outside Bury St Edmunds. The King of Scots was captured at Alnwick. The Earl of Chester sued for peace. Louis VII proved no match for Henry II in war. By the autumn of 1174, after eighteen months of fighting, England and France were once again pacified. Now, however, the peace was entirely dictated by John's father. Not only were his enemies humiliated, but a great number of castles now fell into the king's hands. For the first time since the Norman Conquest of 1066, the kings of England became masters of a majority of the castles in England.

What did John learn from these events? Perhaps that, in an extreme situation, defiance was always preferable to appeasement. Moreover, at moments of crisis, to distinguish the loyal from the rebellious it was sometimes necessary to provoke the discontented into open revolt. In practical terms, the rebellion of 1173–4 had other consequences for John. There was now no question of his being destined for the Church. Moreover, whatever his earlier relations with his mother, Eleanor of Aquitaine, she herself was now entirely removed from his upbringing. As is sometimes the case when a mother is absent or disgraced, and where elder siblings have displayed disobedience (as with John's elder brothers), a bond of affection grew up between father and younger son. John was soon openly regarded as his father's favourite.

There remained the issue of marriage. John's Savoyard fiancée had died within a few months of their betrothal. In her place, in 1176, an English heiress was proposed. Isabella, eldest daughter and heiress of William, Earl of Gloucester, was also John's cousin, which would place their union well within the degrees of kinship requiring special licence from the Church. Earl William had flirted with the rebellion of 1173–4. By agreeing to the betrothal of John and Isabella, he bought his way back into royal favour. The price he paid was to recognize John as heir to his vast estates. The greatest prize here was Earl William's city of Bristol, henceforth John's chief seat of operations. By this time, too, John had begun to acquire other possessions. In 1174, under the treaty ending the civil war, he had been promised a substantial income from rents on both sides of the Channel. Nottingham Castle was set aside for his use. A year later, following the death of the king's uncle Reginald, Earl of Cornwall, John was granted custody of a substantial part of Reginald's inheritance, in effect disinheriting the earl's daughters and illegitimate son.

Both Bristol and Cornwall looked westwards to the trade of the Irish Sea. Ever since his accession, John's father had dreamed of conquering Ireland. His role-model here was the mythical King Arthur. Deliberately popularized at the Angevin court, the legends of Arthur reported not only Arthur's supposed conquests of Ireland and France, but his attempts to seize the empire of Rome through campaigns into Italy: precisely the trajectory on which John and his father had embarked in the 1170s with the prospect of lordship over Turin and the Alpine passes. In 1171–2, and in part to divert attention from his ungodly role in Becket's murder, Henry had crossed to Ireland, imposing a degree of order on the English barons who had recently established authority over the coastal towns of Cork, Waterford, Wexford and Dublin. Henceforth, Dublin and its hinterland, 'the Pale', became an enclave of royal rather than baronial authority.

For a while, Henry II attempted to govern Dublin through proxies. But he had a longer-term goal. As early as 1177, within a year of John's betrothal to Isabella of

Gloucester, Henry II summoned a council to Oxford. There, John was proclaimed the future King of Ireland. For this proclamation to take effect, accommodation had to be sought with the papacy, which, for at least the past four hundred years, had come to regard Ireland as in some senses a papal possession: one of those 'islands of the west' promised to the popes according to the Donation of Constantine. The Donation, in theory a decree of the early fourth century transferring authority over the western Roman Empire to the Pope, was in reality a forgery first brought into debate from the eighth century onwards. Its authenticity, however, went largely unchallenged into the 1450s and beyond.

Meanwhile, John's Irish crown remained an aspiration, conferring no hard power. In particular, John still had no real property of his own, not even in England, where he was granted the revenue from lands, not possession of land itself. Like many favourite sons, John had gained the affection of his father but also a degree of paternal mockery and contempt. As we have noted, Henry's court was a place of cruel verbal humour. By the early 1180s, in a nickname coined by his father, John was openly described as 'John Lackland'. The nickname stuck.

In 1183, Earl William of Gloucester died, in prison, so it was reported, suspected of involvement in yet another conspiracy among Henry II's rebellious sons. John now became custodian of the entire earldom of Gloucester, a vast collection of castles, manors and military tenancies straddling the Severn estuary as far west as Cardiff and including significant estates in Normandy, themselves with easy access

to the sea. Here were the foundations of a maritime lordship to which Ireland could be joined. The same year,
John's seventeenth, also witnessed the collapse of a further
rebellion in France with the death of John's eldest brother,
Henry. Styled King of England even in his father's lifetime,
this Henry 'the Young King' had been a glamorous but
politically incompetent playboy – darling of the tournament field, feted as a celebrity across Western Europe, yet
never permitted real authority. His death brought John
a step closer to the throne, an advance redoubled in 1186
when another of his brothers, Geoffrey, Duke of Brittany,
was trampled to death in a tournament outside Paris. From
this point onwards, and in the absence of any sign that his
only surviving elder brother, Richard, would father an heir,
John 'Lackland' was never more than a heartbeat away from
kingship.

To prove his fitness to rule, and, aged eighteen, fast
approaching his majority, John crossed to Ireland in 1185.
Our knowledge of this expedition comes almost exclusively
from a single chronicle, written by an embittered and hence
untrustworthy clergyman, Gerald of Wales.[4] Gerald's is
an account deliberately hostile to John. Most notoriously,
according to Gerald, shortly after his arrival at Waterford,
John allowed members of his court to mock the native
Irish, and even to tug on their long, shaggy beards. Youth-
ful folly, Gerald hints, rendered the entire expedition a
failure. Far from subduing the Irish, or acknowledging the
rights of the veteran Englishmen already settled there, John
rewarded only his young followers, ignoring those with
local military experience. The effect was to isolate the

cities of the Irish coast from inland regions now entirely given over to resistance. John's money and resources were squandered to no good effect. John himself returned to England in December 1185, to be presented with a coronet of gold and peacock feathers sent to him by the Pope: an empty gesture, it has been suggested, no real substitute for the Irish crown that he had originally sought.

There is much in this account that is biased or misleading. Modern historians have scoffed at John's peacock coronet, without realizing that a crown of peacock feathers was a symbol very specifically identified with triumph and military conquest. It was just such a 'tufa' or tuft of peacock feathers that the emperors of Byzantium wore on returning from successful campaigns. By sending a peacock crown, the Pope was honouring John, not scorning him. Historians have also ignored the twenty or more land grants recorded in letters that John issued while in Ireland. These tell a story very different from that recounted by Gerald. Here we find the young John deliberately, and with a fair degree of skill, building up both a personal entourage and a future administrative elite. It was under John, in 1185, that English and Norman families such as the Burghs, the Verduns and the Butlers first gained land in Ireland: for the next several centuries the mainstays of England's colonial administration.

Nor did John shirk his military responsibilities, as Gerald alleges. On the contrary, he built castles (at Lismore, Tybroughney and Ardfinnan), as staging points from which to exploit rivalries between the native dynasties of the Irish south-west. Dublin was brought under the economic oversight of the men of Bristol, with potential commercial benefits to John. Land was assigned in the southern Irish kingdoms of Desmond and Munster on a deliberately speculative basis, granting away estates that had still to be conquered from the Irish. But there was sound sense here, not least in discouraging what might otherwise have been a free-for-all land-grab by men with no personal attachment to John. Far from being a chaotic or disastrous failure, John's 1185 expedition in reality laid the basis both for future English conquests beyond the immediate vicinity of Dublin, and for the role of Dublin itself as the colony's capital.

All of this speaks of competence matched to ruthless self-interest. But there was a darker side. John was a mere ten years old when he was first promised Ireland, and still only eighteen when he took possession of the colony in 1185. Much has been written about his impact upon Ireland. But what impact did Ireland have upon the future King John? Was it here, for example, that John acquired his later obsession with hostage-taking? Hostages were a fundamental aspect of Irish politics, and in Ireland, unlike England or France, they were regularly and brutally killed in reprisal for breaches of a peace impossible for either native or invading Englishmen to maintain. John, as we shall see, was to earn notoriety for his killing or prolonged incarceration of hostages.

Was it also in Ireland that John acquired his taste for collecting the heads of his enemies as trophies, later notorious in his dealings with the Welsh, but already apparent as early as the 1180s, according to Gerald of Wales? Was it in these same circumstances that he acquired his equally notorious delight in watching judicial duels – the ritual battles between accused and accuser in which one party, favoured by God, would batter the other to death? Certainly, and by contrast to English practice, jurisdiction over duels and ordeals was regularly bestowed in John's Irish charters as a privilege of the greater settler lords. It is in a case involving a murder at Dublin Castle that John is first found insisting that he attend the resulting duel. Moreover, this case, from the 1190s, supplies not only our earliest reference to the building of the great ditch of Dublin Castle – a feat of slave labour equivalent to or greater than William the Conqueror's building of the Tower of London – but our clearest proof that it was under John as lord of Ireland, perhaps as early as 1185, that English judicial procedures were first carried across the Irish Sea.[5]

Above all, was it in Ireland, with its warring native kings and its clannish network of lordships, liberties and honours, that John first perfected his divide-and-rule strategy towards the barons? We find this strategy already in place in Ireland as early as the 1180s and 1190s. It was to surface again many times thereafter, with profound effects upon John's relations with his subjects not only in Ireland, but in Normandy and England. In the process, John introduced to Anglo-French politics techniques mastered in the far harsher circumstances of Irish colonial warfare. John was perhaps that most remarkable, indeed unique of creatures: a king of England first trained to kingship in Ireland. The problem for his subjects was not that John failed to organize effective lordship for the Irish. The problem was

that John became too Irish for his French or English subjects to bear.

To this extent, although misleading in detail, Gerald of
Wales was right to signal concerns over John's time in Ireland. There was already, as early as 1185, a sense that not
all boded well for his future career as king, whether in
Ireland or elsewhere. Such misgivings were to multiply
over the coming decade. In 1189, when Henry II once again
faced rebellion in France, the king's death is reputed to
have been hastened by news that John's name headed the
list of those secretly leagued in rebellion with King Philip
of France. Thereafter, with the accession of John's elder
brother, Richard 'the Lionheart', doubts as to John's reli-
ability continued to surface.

King Richard began his reign with generosity towards
his younger brother. After more than a decade of betrothal,
John was at last permitted to marry Isabella of Gloucester
and thereby gain full possession of her estate. He was
also granted custody of at least six English counties, from
Cornwall and Somerset, via Nottingham to Lancaster. In
Normandy, he was recognized as Count of Mortain, ruler
of one of the great Norman honours or landed estates originally created for a kinsman of William the Conqueror.
With its port at Montmartin-sur-Mer, just north of Mont-
Saint-Michel, the county of Mortain occupied a crucial
position both as a lynchpin of the Plantagenet empire in
France and as a part of that great seaborne condominium
now controlled by John: a network of key ports, from
Montmartin via Bristol, Cardiff, Dublin and now Lancaster, straddling the entire western seaboard of Richard's

kingdom. In all of this there was an implicit recognition that Richard – unmarried and with no legitimate son to succeed him – had chosen John as his heir. The last person before John to control such a combination of honours including Mortain and Lancaster had been Stephen of Blois, crowned in 1135 as successor to John's great-grandfather, King Henry I.

Yet there were complications. Although he had no son by marriage, Richard none the less had a young nephew, Arthur of Brittany, born on Easter Sunday 1187, eight months after the death of his father – Richard and John's brother Geoffrey. This circumstance ensured that there was no clear line of succession. Rather, there would henceforth be competition between John, as Richard's younger brother, and Arthur, Richard's nephew by a brother older than John and therefore higher in the line of succession. For the next fifteen years, uncertainty as to whether John or Arthur had greater right to the English throne was to remain a corrosive issue both in law and politics. At Richard's accession in 1189, John was twenty-two; Arthur not yet three years old. Not only this, but Arthur was regarded as a potential pawn of England's enemies: the King of France, claiming to act as his overlord for Brittany, and the King of Scots, his mother's uncle. John's seemed by far the stronger claim. Yet as Arthur grew up and John's reputation for untrustworthiness spread, John's hopes for the succession became clouded.

In these circumstances, King Richard did what his Plantagenet ancestors had always done best. He prevaricated. He was about to embark on crusade. It is surely a sign of the lack of any strong personal bond between the brothers that Richard made no attempt to persuade John to accompany him to the East. But neither was John to be trusted with government at home. To begin with, he was made to swear to make no attempt to enter England but instead to remain either in Normandy, or potentially Ireland, for the entire period of Richard's absence. This restriction was then unofficially relaxed, apparently at the request of John's mother, the newly liberated Eleanor of Aquitaine. Instead, in the worst of all possible compromises, John was promoted as one of an ill-matched council of regents, headed by Richard's former confidential clerk, now chancellor and Bishop of Ely, William Longchamp. A Frenchman, and a social upstart, Longchamp never secured the confidence of his fellow regents.

Worse still, as far as John was concerned, Richard at last took decisive steps for his succession. In September 1191, en route for the Middle East and his crusade, he stopped off in Sicily. There he married a young Spanish princess, Berengaria of Navarre, hoping to secure protection for his southernmost lands in France. Second – and pending the birth of any children by Berengaria – he recognized Arthur of Brittany as his heir. The intention here was short-term diplomatic advantage in Richard's dealings with the rulers of France and Sicily, before whom the four-year-old Arthur was dangled as a potential marriage partner. This was achieved only at the cost of an open breach with John.

This was the worst of all possible settlements. In the longer term, Richard's Spanish marriage proved childless; whether or not because Richard himself was homosexual, historians will continue to debate. In England, it provoked uproar between John and William Longchamp. In March 1191, Longchamp laid siege to Lincoln Castle, held against him by a former servant of Henry II. This man, Gerard de Canville, appealed to the protection of John who in turn garrisoned his great fortresses of Nottingham and Tick-hill (near Doncaster). Attempts to broker a peace failed. In October, Longchamp was deposed and forced into exile. Henceforth, should Richard die in the East, John, and not his nephew Arthur, was recognized as heir to the throne. Even so, John himself continued to be denied executive power. This passed instead to the Archbishop of Rouen, ruling in concert with three others: William Marshal, Earl of Pembroke; Hubert Walter, newly elected Archbishop of Canterbury; and in due course the king's mother, Elea-nor of Aquitaine.

Thus far, John had acted deviously and provocatively but not treasonably. All of this changed at the end of 1191, when King Philip of France returned from the East. John now began deliberately to make trouble. He extorted money and the castles of Windsor and Wallingford from the regency council, threatening otherwise to make com-mon cause with his former rival, the disgraced Longchamp. Rumours circulated that he was conspiring with King Philip. Rumour turned to certainty early in 1193, when news arrived of Richard's capture outside Vienna as he returned overland from his crusade. John hurried to Normandy and entered into open alliance with Philip. The chroniclers report that John was promised marriage to Philip's sister, Alice, and advancement to the English throne. The fact that John was already married, to Isabella of Gloucester, seems to have been considered an irrelevance. The hope was clearly that John and Isabella's marriage could be annulled on the pretext of their close kinship.

When a treaty between John and Philip was eventually sealed, in January 1194, it revealed an extraordinary naivety on John's part. John promised to cede to Philip the whole of Normandy east of the River Seine, retaining only the city of Rouen. Elsewhere, entire regions, including the cities of Évreux, Tours and Angoulême, were to be detached from the Plantagenet dominion and handed to Philip, who in return would receive John's homage for what remained. The effect here would have been to dismember Henry II's empire, indeed the entire Anglo-French settlement established since the Norman Conquest of 1066. All of this was not only miscalculated but proved pure moonshine, since by January 1194 Richard was on the verge of release from captivity.

In England, the regency council had struggled to raise the vast sum of 100,000 marks (£66,666) demanded as Richard's ransom by the German emperor. In February 1194, John himself was excommunicated by the English bishops and his castles placed under siege. Richard landed at Sandwich in March. By the end of the month, he had not only taken personal surrender of Nottingham, the last of John's rebellious garrisons, but commanded John's banishment. In less than eight weeks from his landing in England, Richard was in a position to return to Normandy. There, in a humiliating settlement brokered by Queen Eleanor, John knelt before Richard, begging forgiveness. His lands and castles remained forfeit to the crown.

Yet Richard had so low an opinion of John that he still refused to regard him as a serious threat. Warned of John's treachery as early as 1193, he had dismissed the danger, claiming that his brother was not the sort of man to resist firm opposition. More extraordinarily still, within a year of his disgrace, John was rehabilitated and restored to a degree of control over his estates, including Ireland. John, Richard declared, was 'a mere child'. John in reality was by then twenty-seven years old. In Richard's final years, John campaigned on behalf of his brother in Normandy, even though King Philip continued to warn Richard that John was playing a double game. With Arthur now a permanent fixture at the French court, John was generally regarded as Richard's most likely successor.

Nobody could have expected the sudden death that overtook Richard, on 6 April 1199, struck down by a crossbow bolt while besieging an obscure castle outside the southwestern French city of Limoges. John was hundreds of miles away at the time, in Brittany as a guest of his nephew Arthur. Neither John nor Richard had returned to England since 1194. To this extent, John was as much a stranger to his English subjects as ever Richard had been. He had been absent from his Irish lordship since 1185. Even in Normandy, where he chiefly resided, he had failed to establish any sort of close rapport either with the Norman aristocracy or the Norman Church. Like his father and brother before him, he remained an unstable and menacing presence, permanently in transit, never at rest.

When the news of Richard's death became known, there were some who still hesitated to accept John's claim to the throne. Arthur, for all his friendship with the French, was now twelve years old and fast approaching maturity. John was widely reputed to have failed as lord of Ireland. In 1189 he had betrayed his loving father and in 1193 his crusading brother, despite that brother being placed under the most solemn protection of the Church. In Cornwall, Gloucester and Ireland he had acquired rich lands through marriage and family favour, but only at the expense of dispossessing those who considered themselves the rightful heirs. He was reputed cruel, and even in an age of widespread adultery his extramarital relations were regarded as scandalous. Above all, long before he became king, he was already marked out as an oath-breaker: a man whose word was not to be trusted. In all these respects, as oath-breaker, plunderer of baronial property, as a model of cruelty and sexual excess, John merely aped the pattern already established by his father and elder brother. The irony was that John was to be villainized for doing things that his father and elder brother had done more ruthlessly, yet more effectively. John was never to murder his Archbishop of Canterbury (like Henry II), nor provoke accusations of sodomy (like Richard I). But Henry and Richard won the majority of their wars. John did not. Herein lay the seeds of much future woe. Although he was unaware of the fact, when John succeeded as king, in May 1199 at the age of thirty-two, he was about to lose the empire so painstakingly assembled by his father and elder brother.

2

A Catalogue of Infamy?

John's Reign in France, 1199–1204

In hindsight, things went badly with John's reign from the start. At Rouen, awaiting his crossing to England, he was enthroned as Duke of Normandy. During the ceremony, held in Rouen Cathedral, John was so busy fooling about for the entertainment of his young admirers that he lost concentration and dropped the ducal lance – or so at least it was later reported.[1]

At the time various authoritative figures, including the greatest of Richard's former servants, Hubert Walter, Archbishop of Canterbury, and William Marshal, Earl of Pembroke, were still prepared to throw their weight behind John, arguing vociferously for his claims over those of Arthur of Brittany. It was Hubert who met John in Normandy, immediately after Richard's funeral, escorting him to England and eventually crowning him as king, in Westminster Abbey on Ascension Day, Thursday 27 May 1199.

Even then, there must have been doubts. At Fontevraud, where John went to pay his respects to his newly buried brother, there was a peculiar exchange in which the saintly Hugh, Bishop of Lincoln, attempted to remind John of his duties towards God. Not only did John mock such scruples, but he showed the bishop a precious jewel, hung around his neck, with whose aid, he claimed, he would never lose his ancestral estates. There had been a further such scene at Mass on Easter Sunday, when John very publicly hesitated before placing the customary gold coins on the altar as his royal offering. Not only this, but he commanded, three times, that the bishop cut short his sermon so that John and his cronies could dine.[2] This was a king who publicly scoffed at religion. But what was anyone to do? Other than Arthur, rejected by the English court, what alternative was there to John? This was by no means the first (nor the last) occasion when hereditary right, or even free election, produced a leader deemed less than perfect by his contemporaries. But precisely how imperfect was this new king to be?

Having been crowned at Westminster, John embarked on the customary round of pilgrimages, visiting the great shrines of Bury St Edmunds and Canterbury. On the surface, at least, this was intended to be an ordinary inauguration of what many must already have feared would be a far from ordinary reign. Contemporaries took note, however, that neither on Easter Sunday nor at the feast of the Ascension, the day of his coronation, did the king receive the sacraments at Mass. At Bury, where he was expected to deposit rich gifts, he left behind nothing but twelve pence and a silk cloth, itself borrowed for the occasion from the Bury monks.

John's first concern as king was clearly Normandy. In 1194, in the midst of the rebellion against Richard, the French king, Philip, had recovered the border lands immediately to the west of Paris, the so-called 'Vexin', shifting the balance of power very firmly in favour of the French. Not only this, but through inheritance and purchase, Philip's kingdom was also expanding northwards, towards Amiens and the sea. With this came an exponential increase in the French king's financial resources. Put simply, Philip now had more land, and hence more money, with which to prosecute war. John had rather less. In order to bolster his ailing dukedom, John headed for Normandy. He would spend the lion's share of his first five years as king (forty-four of his first fifty-five months) in France, either in Normandy or on the Loire.

John's intention was to prove himself as effective a protector of the Normans as Henry or Richard had been before him. Happily for John, King Philip had problems of his own. His marriage, in 1193, to the Danish princess Ingeborg, had gone catastrophically wrong: after a single night, Philip repudiated his bride and took a mistress. Whatever the explanation here – physical deformity, sorcery, halitosis have all been suggested – Philip placed himself at odds with the Church. As a result, from January to September 1200, a new and ambitious young Pope, Innocent III, placed France under 'interdict', forbidding the public celebration of Mass and the Christian burial of the dead. In the midst of this debacle, Philip was persuaded to conclude a treaty with John. Sealed at Le Goulet, in May 1200, on an island in the River Seine, this was intended by John to mark a triumphant climax to his first year as king.

In theory, the treaty offered advantages to both sides. In return for surrendering strategic interests on a newly demilitarized Norman–French frontier, John was promised peaceful possession of his remaining lands. In token of future harmony, Philip's thirteen-year-old son and heir, Louis, was married to John's twelve-year-old niece, Blanche of Castile. John had bought peace, but only at a significant price, reconfirming that he held his lands as a vassal of the King of France, and paying Philip 20,000 marks (£13,333) – a sum that, coming on top of the vast costs of warfare and Richard's ransom, John could ill afford. In the pocket of King Philip, the money was to help finance what would develop into a final push for the French conquest of Normandy. Not only this but by reversing earlier arrangements that John had made with the counts of Boulogne and Flanders and with Otto of Brunswick, claimant to the German Empire, the treaty in effect involved the betrayal of those who had previously been John's closest allies in northern France. Once again, John revealed himself to be both a poor strategist and a breaker of solemn oaths.

With northern France in theory at peace, John was now free to deal with two other difficulties. His own marriage had foundered long ago, perhaps as a result of John's indifference, perhaps because his bride, Isabella of Gloucester, was incapable of bearing children. John's elder brothers, Henry the Young King and Richard, and now John himself, had ruled without legitimate offspring. This was to deprive English kingship not only of male heirs but of the daughters whose marriages were so important to international diplomacy. At this point, if John had died, and assuming the exclusion of Arthur, the English throne would have passed to one or other of the children of John's sisters, sprung from the dynasties of Toulouse (Occitan-speaking), Brunswick (German) or Castile (Spanish): a bizarre consequence of the lack of any Anglo-Norman heir in the male line. Not only this, but with attention focused on Normandy and the north, there was a need to supply protection for the southern frontiers of the Angevin lands in France. It was this that had drawn Henry II into marrying his daughter to the King of Castile, and Richard I to seek a bride from Navarre. The risk was that these Spanish in-laws would now turn against the Plantagenets and launch claims of their own to territory north of the Pyrenees.

It was in these circumstances, during the opening months of his reign, that John obtained an annulment from his marriage to Isabella of Gloucester. He then embarked on a search for a new bride. He looked first to Portugal, a useful counterfoil to the threat from Spain, sending envoys to the Portuguese court to obtain a daughter of King Sancho I. While this embassy was still on the road, however, and at grave risk to his ambassadors, John suddenly learned of the availability of an heiress from south-western France. Isabella of Angoulême was the only child of Ademar, Count of Angoulême. Together with his kinsman the Viscount of Limoges, Count Adomar controlled territory crucial for communications between Poitou and Gascony. This was an area never fully brought under Plantagenet lordship. Indeed, it had been in his attempts to secure this region that King Richard had been killed a few months before. Besides the risk to his ambassadors in Portugal, there were two further obstacles to John marrying Isabella of Angoulême. The first was that she was in theory already betrothed, to a local lord, Hugh de Lusignan, Count of La Marche. The second was that this betrothal had itself been prolonged for at least the past two years, almost certainly because Isabella was considered too young to marry. In 1200, she was perhaps only eight or nine years old.[3]

Where Hugh de Lusignan had feared to tread, King John trod boldly, marrying Isabella at Angoulême in August 1200, within only a few weeks of his treaty with France. From Gascony, he then accompanied her to England. There she was crowned queen, at Canterbury, on 25 March 1201: the feast of the Annunciation of the Virgin Mary, peculiarly appropriate to a young maiden expected to supply England with a royal heir. John then returned to France and in June 1201 made what was supposed to be a triumphant visit to King Philip in Paris. Lodged in Philip's palace and plied with wine and rich gifts, John's intention was to cement the alliance made at Le Goulet, a year earlier. In fact, he achieved the precise opposite. Publicly polite, the French mocked John and his courtiers in private, not least for drinking the worst wine in Philip's cellars, leaving the best vintages untouched. Having taken receipt of the 20,000 marks promised since 1200, Philip almost immediately made common cause with John's enemies.

Hugh de Lusignan appealed to Philip against Isabella's abduction. Philip, looking for excuses to reopen hostilities with John, supported these complaints. He also stirred up rebellion by Arthur of Brittany. Throwing off his dependence upon King John, Arthur was betrothed to Philip's daughter Marie. He was also knighted, recognized as

Duke of Normandy and Aquitaine, and promised that any land he might seize from John's estate would be considered his by right of conquest: precisely the same 'right' by which John's ancestors had first seized both Normandy and England. John's marriage thereby became the justification for an act of aggression unlike anything that Philip had risked against John's predecessors Henry II or Richard I.

With the help of his southern French allies, Arthur hurled himself against John's forces and, within a matter of weeks, came close to capturing the king's mother, Eleanor of Aquitaine, besieged at Mirebeau, north of Poitiers. At this point, John took perhaps the greatest risk of his life. In early August 1202, he made a lightning raid south from Normandy. Riding more than two hundred miles in less than three days, he surprised Arthur outside the walls of Mirebeau, capturing the entire rebel force. This was arguably the greatest achievement of John's reign. It was rapidly followed by his most catastrophic error.

Held captive – first at Falaise, later at Rouen – Arthur disappeared. By the winter, sinister rumours were circulating. Some said that John had sent an assassin to kill, blind or castrate his nephew; others that, enraged and possibly drunk, the king himself had murdered Arthur, battering him to death with a stone, then ordering the fifteen-year-old's body to be dumped into the River Seine. Whatever the truth, when demands were raised for John to produce his captive, he either failed or was unable to do so. He also refused repeated summons from his sovereign lord in France, King Philip. Proclaiming him in contempt of court,

Philip sentenced John to forfeit his entire French estate, not just in Normandy but as far south as the Pyrenees. This process was itself highly irregular. Where kings of England in the past had used rebellion or conspiracy to justify the seizure of baronial lands, the kings of France had been too timid, or too righteous, to employ such tactics. In 1203, Philip took a leaf out of the Plantagenet book, imposing on John the same rough justice that John and his ancestors had previously imposed upon their own rebellious vassals.

Fearing French attack, John spent a large part of 1203 close to his key base at Rouen. The avoidance of battles was an established technique in medieval warfare. Battles were always dangerous affairs whose outcome could all too easily be distorted by accident and the unexpected. Indeed, it was precisely in their avoidance of pitched battles that both Henry II and Richard had earned their formidable reputations as military commanders. As so often, by attempting to follow their examples, John merely drew attention to his own inadequacy. Where Henry or Richard would surely have remained at the gates of Rouen defending their territory to the last inch, John fled.

That December, at the last possible moment for safe passage across the English Channel, John took ship to England. Exhaustion perhaps explains this flight: the king's personal exhaustion; exhaustion of his financial resources; and above all the exhaustion of his Norman subjects, who for the past ten years had fought a near-continuous war on the Norman frontier, with all of the attendant destruction of crops and property. Normandy, perhaps, grew tired of

John just as John himself tired of Normandy. To contemporaries, however, there was no doubt that John's flight was a shameful thing. The old nickname, 'Lackland', that his father had first bestowed on him now came easily to the tongues of those such as the courtier Baldwin de Béthune, said to have berated John in 1204, telling him to 'be quiet, my lord, you landless wretch!' (literally, 'you rogue without heritage').[4] To this was now added the even more contemptuous, and sexually charged nickname 'Softsword' – a damning indictment of John's perceived lack of virility.[5]

Even in John's absence, Normandy might still have been held against French invasion. Vast sums of money had been lavished on its castles, not least on the great fortress at Château Gaillard, intended to protect Rouen from attack along the Seine Valley. Further south, the Plantagenet lands bristled with defences. Yet with the king now seen as having abandoned his French lands, resistance crumbled. Château Gaillard fell in March 1204, followed by the ducal capitals at Caen and Rouen. At Château Gaillard and elsewhere there were accusations of treachery against those who surrendered, John masking his own shame by blaming his subordinates. When, that June, Rouen fell to the French, John was at his favoured hunting lodge at Gillingham in Dorset. There, on more or less the same day that Rouen surrendered, he and his court consumed a dozen casks of the best French and Angevin wine.[6]

From Normandy, the armies of Philip threatened to sweep away the entire Angevin empire. Le Mans, Angers and Tours all fell to the French. So in due course did Poitiers. The few garrisons that remained, as at Loches, south of Tours, capitulated within a year. But then the tide ebbed. Philip and the French were too busy harvesting the spoils of victory to pursue their conquests further south. An opportunistic invasion of Gascony in 1205 by the King of Castile petered out at Bordeaux, leaving the Spaniards to retrace their steps across the Pyrenees. The Gascons, always the most remote of the subjects of the Plantagenet kings, preferred the distant John as their ruler, rather than accept the far more immediate lordship either of Castile or France. So too did Angoulême and the great port of La Rochelle, midway between Bordeaux and the Loire. With La Rochelle at his disposal, John could still dream of reconquering his lost lands. In June 1206, using La Rochelle as his entry point, he led an expedition to his southern lands, patrolling the western seaboard from the Garonne as far north as Angers. Although modest in its achievements, this expedition at least signalled the possibility of a more permanent return.

Philip's conquest of 1204 was by no means the first occasion since 1066 when England and Normandy had been severed. Looking to the examples of history, John and his advisers may have been reasonably optimistic of a rapid reconquest. Earlier losses by England's kings had proved temporary, with the English always returning to their Norman dominions. But such optimism was, now, to prove short-lived. Why this sudden break in the pattern after 1204? To begin with, in 1204 Normandy was conquered not by some rogue member of the Anglo-Norman royal family, disputing the claims of his brothers or cousins, but by John's overlord in Normandy, Philip,

King of France. Philip followed legal process and seized lands formerly held by a rebellious subject widely suspected of murder. Second, there was John's reaction. Whenever in the past English kings had been ejected from their Norman lands, the outcome had been civil war, spilling over into England. But after the fiasco of 1204, no such war erupted. In part this reflected general war-weariness among the Anglo-Norman elite. But it was also because, as a result of deliberate planning and the division of landed estates over recent generations, most of the greater Anglo-Norman families were already clear as to where their chief interests lay, in England or in Normandy. Only at the very top of society did landholders – such as the earls of Gloucester or Pembroke, and above all the royal family itself – suffer significant losses as a result of the French invasion of Normandy. To compensate such losses, a system of confiscations was devised. Mirroring Philip of France's confiscation of Norman lands belonging to English subjects, John now confiscated the English lands of those who adhered to the King of France.

The result, for John, was a windfall: the largest collection of land annexed by the crown at any time between 1066 and Henry VIII's dissolution of the monasteries in the 1530s. These lands could be used to compensate the king and his followers. At the same time, although in theory held temporarily by the crown pending the English reconquest of Normandy, such estates in fact served as a positive disincentive to reconquest. For those who grew rich from confiscated land, the last outcome wished for was a reunification of England and Normandy, with its threatened restoration of pre-conquest property rights. Only the king, and a small minority of French or Anglo-Norman landholders now stranded in England, continued to press strongly for Normandy to be reconquered.

The outcome was a massive rupture: perhaps the greatest redistribution of Anglo-French resources at any time between 1066 and Britain's proposed departure from the European Union announced in 2016. As after 2016, so after 1204 particular concerns focused upon the fate of Frenchmen now stranded in England. The king's close coterie of French mercenaries and constables, hopelessly compromised by their service in France, sought asylum across the English Channel, finding employment in the English provinces as sheriffs and constables. In this way Girard d'Athée, from Athée, east of Tours, one-time constable of Loches, became Sheriff of Gloucester and Herefordshire. His kinsmen and associates Philip Marc, Engelard de Cigogné and Peter, Guy and Aimery de Chanceaux, all from the same region of the Loire, were promoted as sheriffs in Nottinghamshire, Bristol and the Welsh Marches.

A few of these exiled Frenchmen rose by marriage to control major English estates. One, Peter de Maulay, was granted marriage to the heiress to a Yorkshire barony together with the castles of Doncaster and Mulgrave; another, Philip d'Aubigny, a native of Brittany, added to his English estates by marrying an heiress from Kent. Foreign clerks, meanwhile, were richly rewarded with ecclesiastical patronage, none more so than Peter des Roches. A former servant of King Richard, from the vicinity of Tours, Peter was promoted in 1205 as Bishop of Winchester, ruler of the richest diocese in Europe north of Milan. In this way, John came to rely on an inner circle of French cronies, at precisely the same time that 'the French' more generally were being vilified in England for their victories over John in France. By such means, in attempting to strengthen the prospects for reconquest, John alienated the English barons upon whom such reconquest chiefly depended.

3
From the Frying Pan into the Fire
John's Reign in England, 1204–14

At no time in its history has England severed links with the continent without serious disturbance: in the fourth century, after the departure of the Romans; in the 1450s, after defeat in the Hundred Years War; after the loss of Calais in 1558; even after disengagement following victories in 1815, 1918 and 1945. In each case, the times that followed have tended to be characterized by hardship, paranoia and unease. There could be no doubt that in 1204 King John had suffered a shameful defeat in France. In the immediate term, however, the dimensions of that defeat were masked first by the prospect of reconquest, then by the redistribution of confiscated lands in England, and thereafter by the failure of the disgruntled to agree to any concerted course of action against the king. The sheer extent of English royal authority, cemented since the last great rebellion of the 1170s, and reinforced by the lack of any younger brothers or cousins capable of cultivating rebellion, ensured that John passed into the second phase of his reign superficially unscathed.

Now, though, where John had previously been absent from England – spending only eleven of the first fifty-five months of his reign on English soil – he became all too constant a presence. The English barons, many of whom expected relief and relaxation after decades of near-constant French wars, found themselves menaced by a king no longer thundering his commands from the banks of the Seine or the Loire, but on their own back doorsteps, travelling England with manic energy, determined upon his own selfish purposes. Far from a lull after the storm, there followed a decade overshadowed by two related crises. The first was financial, provoked by taxation to pay for reconquest. The second focused upon John's deteriorating relations both with the English barons and with the English Church.

England was a wealthy land, perhaps the wealthiest in medieval Europe. It possessed a currency, 'sterling', whose silver content was higher than that of all other Christian realms. This in turn reflected the strength of English exports, above all of wool. English wool was finer in quality and was produced in greater quantity than could be obtained elsewhere. As a result, a great river of silver flowed into England from foreign trade, recoined as sterling in a process that for centuries had been carefully manipulated to the profit of England's kings. Not only this but long before 1066, in response to the threat of foreign invasions from Vikings, Frenchmen or Flemings, England's kings had developed tax-raising powers that were the envy of all other European monarchies.

Under John's father, the ancient system of 'geld' collection (a land tax to pay for national defence) had been replaced by taxes more directly related to military service, and in particular by a payment known as 'scutage' – literally 'shield money' – payable by those unable or unwilling to serve in the king's army, who instead sent money for the king to hire mercenaries. Collected from the greater lay and ecclesiastical barons, according to the number of knights who were in theory established on their estates, this was a payment passed down by the barons to their knights. Provided that a baron had more knights established on his lands than he was liable to answer for to the crown, each time that a scutage was taken both the king and the baron stood to gain. A baron who collected £1 from a hundred knights but owed scutage for only fifty thus reaped a profit of £50.

Besides scutage, the king claimed the right to take more extensive taxes from his subjects. Some of these were customary, imposed to pay for the knighting of the king's eldest son, the marriage of his eldest daughter (both of these eventualities last experienced in the reign of Henry II) and the ransom of the king's own body, as with the 100,000 marks required to purchase Richard I's release from captivity in Germany. Others were in theory voluntary or 'gracious' payments, subject to negotiation between king and subjects – as in the 1180s and again in 1201, when taxes were imposed to pay for crusades to the Holy Land. In 1200, a land tax was used to raise the 20,000 marks promised to King Philip, and in 1203 John imposed a special tax of a seventh (in effect, a property tax of 14 per cent) to meet the costs of war in France. Provided that a king was seen to be working for the good of his subjects for what contemporaries would have considered public 'necessity', consent to such taxes – whatever grumbling they provoked – was more or less guaranteed. Kings in the past had little difficulty in arguing that national 'necessity' was synonymous with their own private interests.

Beyond his role as tax-gatherer the king was an immensely wealthy landowner in his own right. Each year, from his landed resources administered by the sheriffs on a county by county basis, and from his rights over towns, markets and trade, King John could expect an annual cash income approaching £5,000. To this, he could add a great deal more from the profits of justice: the fines and bribes paid for the administration of the law. Because of both the financial and political advantages here, from the 1150s onwards it was the king's courts and the king's judges who increasingly decided lawsuits, including the most lucrative property cases that might previously have been decided by the barons in their own baronial courts. To the profits of justice were added the traditional spoils of war, from conquest and pillage, and also the incidental profits of 'feudal' lordship, from the administration of the estates of orphans and widows, and the confiscation (or 'escheat') of land whose lord had rebelled or died, leaving no immediate heir. All told, by the beginning of John's reign, kings of England had a more or less guaranteed annual cash income approaching £25,000.

But here came the rub. In theory, it was the ambition of every king to 'live off his own': to balance the books from his own landed income without resorting to extraordinary measures, such as taxation, or risking bankruptcy. In practice, few if any kings achieved this ambition. In King John's case, there were special circumstances. First, rather than profit from war, John was regularly defeated by the French. This in itself might not have proved disastrous: as with later British empires, the costs to England of maintaining the king's overseas possessions almost certainly outstripped the profits. In due course, there should have been a massive cost-benefit from the English withdrawal from Normandy. In reality, however, John committed himself to reconquest in France on a scale that negated any potential saving. He needed to pay not only for an expeditionary force but also for a fleet to transport it, and for expensive local alliances to support his landing. Not only this, but the costs of war extended to the disruption of cross-Channel trade, and hence, potentially, a damaging decline in the wool exports that supplied England's chief source of foreign silver.

Beyond this lay wider macro-economic realities that are still hotly debated. In the 1970s, at a time when rising commodity prices and monetary inflation were predominant concerns, it became fashionable to blame all of King John's problems on a 'great inflation' that supposedly engulfed Western Europe between the 1180s and 1220s. In essence, while the king's lands, leased out to the sheriffs at fixed 'farms' (or land rentals) accrued little or no new profit, the costs of hiring knights doubled or even tripled. The effect was to squeeze royal income. This in turn obliged the king to adopt highly unpopular measures to raise income, either by direct management of his own estates or through taxation, the exploitative sale of custody over orphans or widows, and other such 'feudal incidents' (i.e. incidental benefits of feudal lordship). John, in this interpretation, was not so much the villain as the victim of financial pressures beyond his own control.[1]

The problem here, as with so many macro-economic explanations, is that the economists are unable to agree upon either causes or effects. The origins of the 'great inflation' have still not been fully explained. Some suggest a vast increase in the supply of silver, perhaps from the mines of the Harz Mountains in northern Germany. Others, on the contrary, suggest a silver 'famine' as income from wool exports was disrupted by warfare and the net export of bullion to France. While the cost of hiring knights undoubtedly increased, modern scholars examining the prices of other commodities, such as grain, have detected no steady upwards trend, but rather the ongoing wild fluctuations of prices in an agricultural economy incapable either of predicting year-on-year yields or of hoarding in times of plenty against future periods of dearth.

At least one thing is clear. The greater baronial landholders, capable of resuming control over resources previously leased at unprofitable rents, reaped rewards that far outstripped those of the lesser knights. If a rising economic tide lifts all ships, the ships of the rich nevertheless rise a great deal higher than those of others. In this scenario, baronial wealth multiplied with fewer of the constraints that restricted the wealth of the king. John's was an age of oligarchs. Post-Soviet Russia, or the Blair and Thatcher years in British history, supply some indication of what can happen when the previously stagnant resources of the rich are suddenly released in full spate. They also suggest ways in which rising affluence is often coupled with insecurity and a sense of impending doom. Combine this with defeat in foreign wars, and the results could prove as toxic as they did for King John.

By 1204, John had already imposed five scutages and three direct taxes in only five years. Something in excess of £35,000 had been collected by these means. Yet not a single military victory could be claimed. Not only had John lost vast estates in France, but his preoccupation with Anglo-French warfare excluded England from the Fourth Crusade of 1202–4. Englishmen keen to emulate the heroic chivalry of Richard I had no outlet for their ambitions nor any role to play in the great bonanza of 1204 when the crusaders sacked Constantinople, releasing a vast tide of plunder to those, mostly French or Flemish, who took part.

The end of war in France should have spelled the end of taxation to pay for war. Instead, in 1205, a year after losing Normandy, the king collected the heaviest scutage yet imposed, to finance a campaign in southern France led by mercenary soldiers rather than by John in person. When the king did cross to La Rochelle in 1206, he imposed yet another scutage, taking more than £10,000 all told in less than two years. All of this to pay for a campaign of containment that could claim no real victories, in a part of southern France where the English barons had never held land. On his return to England, John imposed yet another direct tax, this time on movable wealth, calculated as a thirteenth (7.69 per cent), raising at least £60,000. Not only was this the highest such tax yet collected, but it was linked to no specific military project. Instead, it was targeted at a campaign overseas, to be launched whenever the king himself might deem fit. By 1207, there were many English barons who neither longed for reconquest in France nor believed that John was capable of accomplishing it.

In 1209, amid diplomatic negotiations but without any military campaign, scutage was collected for an army to be sent against the Scots. In 1210, the heaviest of all John's scutages, assessed at £2 per knight's fee and raising nearly £8,500, was imposed for a campaign in Ireland. John's own private playground, Ireland remained an 'overseas' colony in which very few of the English barons possessed estates. A scutage of nearly £4,000 was taken for war in Wales in 1211. Scotland, Ireland and Wales, like France to a majority of Englishmen, were regions of only tangential concern. All of these taxes, supposedly justified by necessity, were in fact imposed for the king's own advantage, to mask the king's humiliation and to shore up an empire that he himself had imperilled.

Even had John been a conventionally successful king, victorious in war and ruling with justice, relations with his English barons would always have been strained. The predatory nature of kingship, competition for the profits of land and justice, and the monarch's determination to spend English money on his own French and Irish adventures, all ensured that kings and barons agreed on few things, save perhaps for the need for effective defence against invasion. Even so, the odds were stacked in favour of the king. John commanded landed resources and an annual income in excess of £25,000. He had at his disposal castles and local officials in every one of the English counties. His military establishment, of constables, mercenaries, crossbowmen, and household knights, dwarfed anything that an individual baron could muster. To this John, following Richard, added a powerful fleet operating out of Portsmouth, capable of transporting armies as far east as the Holy Land and, in time of war, not only of blockading the Channel but of shipping mercenaries from France or Ireland to suppress domestic unrest.

By contrast, only a small handful of the very wealthiest of John's subjects, men such as the earls of Chester or the bishops of Winchester, commanded annual incomes even a tenth as high as that of the king. Beneath this upper elite, perhaps thirty barons boasted incomes approaching £1,000 a year. Even if such men combined in opposition, their collective wealth came nowhere near that of the crown. Moreover, the barons were by no means a homogeneous group. Not only were they divided between clergy and laymen, each of these constituencies with its own particular obsessions, but baronial power remained intensely regional, each baron competing for local power and resources not only against the crown but more often against his baronial neighbours. It took a great deal to embolden such men to rebel.

The risks confronted by rebels were enormous: not only confiscation of land and castles, but potentially imprisonment or even loss of life. If the fate of Arthur of Brittany supplied the French with an excuse to invade Normandy, it also demonstrated all too clearly what might happen to a rebel – even one apparently protected by his royal blood – who dared defy the king. What was more, even if the flames of rebellion could be lit, they tended quickly to splutter out. During the last great disturbance, of the 1170s, the rebels had relied upon foreign aid, from France, Flanders and Scotland; not a single English bishop had joined their cause, and the outcome had been humiliation, defeat and a resulting increase in the power of the crown. Not since the 1140s had there existed anything approaching a political coalition among the barons, lay and ecclesiastical, and even in the 1140s this had arisen through the weakness of King Stephen rather than through baronial strength.

It is some measure of John's incompetence that by 1210, and for the first time since the 1140s, baronial opposition began once again to stir. Not only this, but for the first time in more than a generation it brought together earls, bishops and a large number of knights. The knights, as we have seen, were the real victims of scutage and taxation, exploited as much by their baronial overlords as they were by the king. But now, for the first time, we begin to read of political coalitions claiming the support not only of the greater but of the humbler landowners.

We can trace the emergence of opposition through the careers of the two courtiers who had been most crucial to John's accession as king. In 1199, it had been William Marshal, Earl of Pembroke, and, among the bishops, Hubert Walter, Archbishop of Canterbury, who had argued longest and most effectively for John to be chosen over his nephew, Arthur. Hubert died in 1205, less than a year after the fall of Rouen. William Marshal, wrongfooted by the loss of Normandy where many of his more significant resources were situated, negotiated his own private deal with the French. Where in England, Wales and Ireland, the Marshal remained a subject of King John, in Normandy he swore homage to King Philip, thereby guaranteeing his Norman lands but making it impossible for him to campaign against Philip in France on John's behalf. John accused the Marshal of treason. Before retreating to the safety of his Irish lands, the Marshal warned John's courtiers: 'Beware the King: if he gets the upper hand, what he thinks to do with me, he will do to each and every one of you, or even more.'[2]

With the death of Hubert Walter, John perhaps breathed a sigh of relief. 'Now for the first time I am King of England,' he is said to have exclaimed on hearing of Hubert's death.[3] In the longer term, none the less, John was confronted with the perennial difficulty of maintaining royal control over the Church. His relations with the papacy were already complicated. Pope Innocent III had, on the whole, supported John in his struggles with Philip of France. But papal initiatives had proved as ineffective here as they were in attempts to prevent John from promoting his own courtiers to bishoprics in England, Ireland and Normandy. Having bowed to John's bullying early in the reign, the Pope was now determined to make a bolder stand. Innocent had grown up in the aftermath of the great dispute between Henry II and Thomas Becket. Becket's career and martyrdom served as constant reminders not only of the Church's obligation to escape from royal control, but of the wickedness of John and his entire family, as Becket's persecutors. In 1205, the Pope blocked all attempts by the king to promote his own candidate as successor to Archbishop Hubert. Instead, he persuaded the monks of Canterbury to accept an outsider as archbishop.

Besides his English birth, the man chosen by the Pope had virtually nothing to recommend him to King John. His name was Stephen Langton, and, although descended from a minor knightly family from Langton by Wragby near Lincoln, he had been a teacher at the schools of Paris for thirty or more years, in effect as a naturalized French subject. In Paris, he had established a reputation for his exposition of the Bible as a work of history, revealing God's intentions for the Christian faithful, not least through the Bible's many stories of good and bad kings. Langton's Paris pupils had almost certainly included a young Italian named Lothario di Segni: the future Pope Innocent III. These pupils were taught in Langton's lectures that good kings resembled those to be found in France, whereas bad kings, sprung from the dynasty that had murdered Becket, resided in England. Where good kings decreed written laws, in Langton's view, bad kings ruled by appealing to custom and royal right. Where good kings took counsel with their subjects, bad kings ruled as tyrants, misidentifying royal interests as 'necessity'.

Consecrated by the Pope at Viterbo on Trinity Sunday, 17 June 1207, Langton owed his promotion to papal friendship and perhaps to his perceived closeness to the French royal court. A Parisian, he may have been considered a suitable figure to broker peace between the kings of France and England. Instead, and entirely repudiating compromise, his first act as archbishop was to commission a seal to

authenticate his letters. This displayed an image of the martyrdom of Saint Thomas. Becket it was who had first declared
Trinity Sunday to be a feast of the English Church. There
could be no doubt that Langton was claiming to be a
second Becket, persecuted by the son of Becket's chief
enemy, King Henry II. As a result, John had no hesitation
in refusing him entry to England. After a year of increasingly tense negotiations, in March 1208 the Pope placed
England under 'interdict'. For the next six years, the sacraments were in theory forbidden to the Christian faithful:
the closest that the English Church could approach to a
general strike. The king and his court were personally
excommunicated. All but two of the English bishops went
into exile, mostly to France. The dead were not to be buried
in consecrated ground. No church bells were to be rung.
Even in monasteries, where the liturgy of the Mass could
still be recited, it had to be whispered rather than sung.

One of the lessons that John had learned from his father
was that confrontation was sometimes better provoked
than avoided. The papal interdict came into force on Mon-
day 24 March 1208. Having stirred up his ecclesiastical
barons, John now deliberately provoked their secular equivalents. Having already forced William Marshal into exile
in Ireland, he now moved against another great man with
Irish connections. Although twenty years older than the
king, William de Braose was in some ways the closest thing
that the king had to a personal friend. Promoted to rich
estates in England, Wales and Ireland, he had been a member of John's inner circle since the early 1190s: one of a
small band of men who had served John under Richard

and then made the transition into John's royal household. What triggered his disgrace remains uncertain, but one guess is that William was simply too close to John. As a result, he knew too many of John's darker secrets – in particular, the circumstances of Arthur of Brittany's murder. When rumours of the murder began to seep out, the king looked to William, and his wife, Matilda, as the most likely spreaders of scandal.

Like many barons, William owed the king money. Like others in royal favour, he had not previously been expected to repay his debts. These debts none the less loomed over him as a potentially troublesome obligation should his relations with the king deteriorate. In April 1208, a month after the papal interdict was imposed, John met William at Hereford, where William's younger son, Giles de Braose, had been promoted as bishop. There, repayment terms were agreed. William would surrender three of his Welsh castles as a guarantee that he would pay whatever he owed the king. At the same time, he delivered up nephews and vassals as hostages and pledged all his lands in England and Wales as security that his debts would be paid. This was a fatal miscalculation on his part.

John had already begun to intrude his 'alien' French henchman, Girard d'Athée, into the position that William had occupied on the Welsh Marches. Girard now provoked a resentful William into armed resistance. By October 1208, William had fled into Ireland. There he sought refuge with his kinsmen Walter and Hugh de Lacy, lords of Meath and Ulster, the central and northern parts of John's Irish colony. Walter and Hugh were by this time themselves already leagued with the disgraced William Marshal, who was also lord of Leinster, the region around Dublin.

Apart from its physical remoteness from John, Ireland was chosen as a baronial refuge for good reason. It was already a site of resistance against John's policies, its barons harbouring longstanding grievances against him for his campaigns of hostage-taking and divide-and-rule since the 1180s. It was in reaction to such dealings in Ireland, in this instance directed against William Marshal, that we first read, as early as 1207, of collective petitions being addressed to the king, sent in the names of the leading barons of Meath, Ulster and Leinster, including Walter and Hugh de Lacy. While pledging their allegiance to John, the barons demanded that he right wrongs and correct policies to which they objected.

John responded with fury. The Irish, he declared, were claiming the right to make laws without royal permission, 'something unheard of either under us or our ancestors'. Whatever allegiance the barons pledged, he warned, in a phrase dripping with menace, would soon be demanded of them, 'as and when we choose to demand it'.[4]

But while it was one thing for John to defy his enemies, it was quite another for him to threaten his friends. He had already broken with William Marshal and William de Braose, both in theory among the most loyal of the loyal. He now turned his attention to Walter and Hugh de Lacy. In the summer of 1210, a quarter-century after he had last campaigned there, he crossed to Ireland. In late July, he besieged and captured the Lacys' great castle at Carrickfergus. Its entire knightly garrison, the elite of the Lacy tenantry, was thrown into prison. The Lacys themselves fled into exile. Meath and Ulster surrendered to the king. With Braose's lands in Limerick and the west already seized, William Marshal made his peace and was left in possession of Leinster. The entire Irish colony now answered to John. Perhaps this had been the plan all along: a provocation of the Marshal, of Braose, and of the Lacys, the chief men of Ireland, deliberately sparking rebellion that the king could then suppress.

If so, then as a politician John was revealed once again as devious yet naive. Carrickfergus in 1210, like Mirebeau in 1202, should have proved a great victory. Without risking battle, John had triumphed over his enemies. But in Ireland, as at Mirebeau, hubris all too quickly shaded into nemesis. Even before John crossed to Ireland, representatives of William de Braose had sought reconciliation, offering the king the astronomical sum of 40,000 marks (£26,666), more than an entire year of the king's ordinary income, in settlement of William's debts. After Carrickfergus, and having captured William's wife and eldest son as they attempted to flee to Scotland, John used these 40,000 marks as a base calculation, now raised to 50,000 marks (£33,333) to reflect the further trouble to which he had been put.

In return, John promised merely to guarantee the lives of William, his wife and son, without any prospect that William would be restored to his lands. In effect, John was expropriating William's entire estate in settlement of a debt that had begun as a token pledge between friends. When William's wife Matilda admitted that all she had to offer were twenty-four silver marks, two dozen gold coins and fifteen ounces of gold – totalling less than £100 in value – she and her son were imprisoned. William himself fled to France and was outlawed. These details were set out in a royal letter intended to demonstrate that the process against William had been an entirely legitimate affair – conducted according to 'the custom of our realm and the law of the Exchequer'.[5] What the king's letter failed to disclose were the gruesome fates of Matilda and her son.

As with the death of Arthur of Brittany after Mirebeau, precisely what happened after Carrickfergus remains uncertain. All that is known is that Matilda and her son were reportedly starved to death in the king's dungeons, either at Corfe or at Windsor. According to the most detailed report, when their bodies were found, mother and son were locked in a cannibal embrace, Matilda having gnawed away at the boy's cheeks.[6] William de Braose, meanwhile, died in exile in France, buried at the abbey of Saint-Victor in Paris in August 1211, in a ceremony that Archbishop Langton almost certainly stage-managed as public protest against Plantagenet tyranny.

Mirebeau had led directly to John's loss of Normandy. Carrickfergus and the king's persecution of the Braoses supplied a catalyst just as momentous. For the first time, the toxic effects of John's mismanagement of his colonies in Normandy and Ireland began to seep directly into the English political mainstream. William de Braose had never been a popular man. He had been too close to John. In the 1190s, he had been responsible for a notorious massacre on the Welsh Marches. Despite his aristocratic descent, his personal reputation was compromised. Not so that of his wife and son. Matilda, his wife, was the daughter of one of Henry II's most trusted courtiers. Two of her own daughters had secured rich marriages, one to Walter de Lacy, lord of Meath, the other to Robert, Earl of Leicester. William's son, meanwhile, had been married to a daughter of Richard de Clare, Earl of Hertford. The Clares were a family of impeccable lineage, prospering through their dull but regular accumulation of resources rather than through any great wit or intelligence. Richard de Clare seems to have been a plodder rather than a great commander. Even so, if there was any baronial family capable of rivalling the pride and grandeur of the Plantagenets, it was the Clares.

Within the closely intermarried rookery of the Anglo-Norman baronage, the cawing and complaining now spread from branch to branch. Not only this, but for the first time in more than fifty years a coalition began to emerge between aggrieved barons and clergy. Stephen Langton was still an exile in France. So was William de Braose's other son, Giles, Bishop of Hereford. Both attended William's funeral in Paris. Indeed, it was around the bones of William de Braose that the opposition to King John, French, baronial and clerical, may first have coalesced.

The Lacys were also implicated here. As early as 1209, they may have written to the French king, Philip, treasonably offering to stir up rebellion in Ireland. Hugh de Lacy, exiled from Ulster the following year, now joined the military campaign to eliminate heresy in southern France, the so-called Albigensian Crusade, as did Stephen Langton's brother Walter, a Lincolnshire knight.

The crusade itself was led by a northern French baron named Simon de Montfort, heir to the earldom of Leicester previously held by William de Braose's son-in-law, Earl Robert. Simon was a well-respected religious fanatic, a veteran of the Fourth Crusade who had none the less avoided entanglement in the potentially scandalous sack of Constantinople, a Christian city, albeit a city previously placed under Orthodox rather than Roman Catholic rule. For nearly a decade, his claims to a share of the Leicester inheritance had been blocked by King John, suspicious of Simon's connections to the French royal court: rightly, as events were to reveal.

Here was a rich chemical compost of grievance and conspiracy awaiting detonation. The first spark was struck in 1212. The year itself began well for the king. By seizing the resources of the Church, and by continued taxation of his barons, John now commanded a cash treasure greater than anything amassed by his father or elder brother. From the lands of the exiled clergy he had extracted something approaching 100,000 marks. He was said to have imposed extraordinary taxes on the parish clergy, ransoming their mistresses and concubines in mockery of clerical hypocrisy. The Cistercian monks, supposedly the purest of the pure, yet heavily involved in commerce, were just as heavily taxed. So too were the Jews, stripped of their assets in a series of 'tallages' or forced seizures accompanied by threats of violence against anyone reluctant to pay. On his return from Ireland, John was rumoured to have imprisoned the entire Jewish community, knocking out the teeth of one of the greater Jewish money-lenders, Isaac of Norwich, one tooth at a time, day by day, until Isaac contributed to a tallage of more than 60,000 marks.

Neither the Jews nor the Cistercians were popular. Faced with demands for cash, they had little alternative but to call in the debts of those, often Christian knights and barons, who owed them money. Tax a banker and ultimately the bank's customers pay. In the meantime, the king grew rich. His annual income, hovering around £25,000 at the beginning of the reign, mounted as high as £70,000 in 1210, perhaps reaching £100,000 or even £150,000 by 1211.[7] The intention was clear. The king would use his newfound wealth to win back his lands in France. An army and a fleet were commissioned. A series of grand alliances began to form. Lubricated with English silver, these drew in all of the enemies of France: the German Empire in the east, Flanders and Boulogne in the north, Toulouse and Aragon in the distant south. Hundreds of barrels of silver pennies were lodged in the king's provincial treasuries awaiting shipment to France.

But then the clouds began to thicken. In June 1212, strange rumours circulated of disturbances in France ignited by a shepherd boy claiming to carry letters from Christ to King Philip. This, the beginning of the so-called 'Children's Crusade', was merely the first of several wonders that suggested the coming of apocalypse. Fear gripped England. In village after village, horns were heard blown in warning, but of what and by whom nobody was entirely sure. On 11 July 1212, a great fire, started during a 'scotale' or public drinking contest, engulfed London Bridge and much of Southwark south of the Thames. According to one contemporary, where God had punished past sins with the waters of Noah's flood, only London, a new Sodom, merited destruction by fire.[8] On 16 July, a hundred miles north-east of Córdoba, the kings of Christian Spain defeated the Muslim emir of Morocco in the Battle of Las Navas de Tolosa.

The effects of this Spanish victory in England were distant but none the less profound. It was rumoured that King John had previously sought an alliance with the emir, Muhammad al-Nasir. The details of the rumour – that John, at odds with the papacy, proposed to convert to Islam – were far-fetched. Even so, it is entirely plausible that John had negotiated with Morocco, not for his own religious conversion but to support his allies in southern France. There, buoyed up by his victory in Spain and in league with the Count of Toulouse, the King of Aragon was now emboldened to fight back against Simon de Montfort's army crusading against heresy. The Battle of Las Navas was thus followed, just over a year later, by Simon's destruction of the forces of Toulouse and Aragon at the equally decisive Battle of Muret. In this way, events in Spain and the south were to have a significant impact upon John's plans for reconquest in northern France.

In both France and England, meanwhile, there was talk that John would soon be deposed by the Pope, and the English crown be offered to King Philip. Again, while these stories were exaggerated, they none the less reflect a situation in which John had for nearly four years been an excommunicate at odds with the Church. Paranoia fed upon itself. As in other comparable situations (think of the great economic meltdowns of 1929 or 2008), it was to take a decade or so after 1204 for the full effects of John's defeat in Normandy to be felt. The longer delayed, the more poisonous and permanent the effects proved to be.

By August 1212, John was at Nottingham, planning to campaign in Wales. Earlier that summer he had commissioned two special investigations. The first involved something not far short of a new Domesday inquest: a county by county assessment of resources that many must have feared would be used to impose even more draconian royal taxes. The second inquiry was into encroachments on the royal forests, those wide tracts not only of wood but ploughland that covered nearly a quarter of England. In these regions, the rights of private landowners were set aside for the protection of the beasts of the chase, principally deer, and the woods and moorland in which deer lived. Those who poached game or felled trees within the forest were subject to harsh punishment, not only financial but corporal, threatening the loss of life or limb.

Nottingham, in the middle of the kingdom, was a good place from which the king could both hunt and count the profits from his inquests. It was here, instead, that news reached him of conspiracy. His barons, so he was told, planned to kill him, luring him into an ambush in Wales. They would then summon an outsider – perhaps King Philip, perhaps Simon de Montfort, the hammer of heretics – to seize the English throne. The queen, Isabella, and John's sons, Henry and Richard, would be put to death. Some claimed that the queen had already been seized at Marlborough and raped, her youngest son Richard killed and the king's treasure at Bristol seized by foreign invaders.

These rumours spread fast, reported as far away as Cornwall. There a member of John's own bodyguard heard it publicly proclaimed that the king was either dead or a prisoner of the Welsh.[9]

John weathered the storm. Convinced that the chief seat of trouble lay in the north, he made a lightning strike from Nottingham as far north as Durham, outlawing those he identified as the principal conspirators: Eustace de Vescy, lord of Alnwick in Northumberland, and Robert fitz Walter, lord of Dunmow in Essex. Both were well-connected barons: Robert, in particular, was a member of the same Clare affinity as William de Braose, close kin to a dozen or so of the very greatest men in England. Declared outlaws, Eustace and Robert fled to France. There they made common cause with Langton and the exiled clergy. Henceforth whatever protection the Pope granted to the clergy was also extended to Eustace and Robert. The interests of dissident clergy and barons coalesced. Meanwhile John, hoping to buy time and popular sympathy, cancelled his inquests into forests and knights' fees. Instead, he instituted an inquiry into the misdeeds of his sheriffs.

He back-pedalled elsewhere too. Earlier in 1212 he had dealt contemptuously with proposals for peace with the Church. Now, he hastily dispatched an embassy to negotiate in Rome. The outcome was a solemn ceremony conducted near Dover on 22 May 1213, the eve of the feast of the Ascension, the fourteenth anniversary of John's accession as king. Here the king solemnly knelt before the Pope's representative, surrendering England as a feudal possession and promising the Pope an annual tribute, or 'census', for

England and Ireland of 1,000 marks. As these details suggest, John's surrender was not the entirely unprecedented action sometimes suggested. Ireland was already held from the papacy, as John had acknowledged as long ago as 1185 with his peacock crown sent from Rome. Other great islands, not least Sicily and Sardinia, had long acknowledged at least theoretical papal overlordship. In 1204 King Pedro of Aragon and in 1211 the nobles of Portugal had likewise placed themselves under the feudal authority of the Pope. The intention in all of these cases was to obtain the Pope's particular favour and protection.

Although John's reaching out to the Pope was astute, it was not universally approved. Ironically, the most vocal criticisms came from within the Church. English monasteries, especially, were always wary of anything that might justify or extend papal taxation of the English Church. The interests of Rome were by no means invariably synonymous with those of the English clergy, a point that was to be reiterated with even greater insistence over the coming years. Since it was the monasteries, via their chroniclers, who controlled the writing of history, this has inevitably had an impact upon later perceptions of John. Monastic chroniclers took particular delight in reporting the prophecies of a northern hermit, Peter of Wakefield. Towards the end of 1212, Peter began to proclaim that by the coming feast of the Ascension (forty days after Easter), the king would have lost his throne. John was still king on Ascension day 1213, and Peter was condemned to death, according to one account his body tied to a pair of horses and torn apart. But was his prophecy true or false? The chroniclers were uncertain. John was still king, but did he now hold his throne as uncontested sovereign or as a vassal of the Pope?

John's surrender resolved any threat that he might be deposed by the Pope. This in turn delivered a blow to the French king's invasion plans. A great French fleet, more than a thousand ships, was assembled in Flanders that spring. In May 1213, at more or less the same time that John was acting out his surrender to Rome, the king's half-brother William 'Longsword', Earl of Salisbury, attacked the French fleet at the port of Damme, the forerunner of modern Zeebrugge. The fleet was destroyed. King Philip fled, the chroniclers reported, 'without honour'. On 9 July 1213, a Tuesday – no doubt chosen because Tuesdays were especially devoted to the memory of Thomas Becket – Stephen Langton at last entered England. Meeting him in the porch of Winchester Cathedral, John fell at his feet, theatrically begging forgiveness. Placing his hand on the Gospels, he then swore not only to restore whatever goods he had seized from the exiled clergy, but to protect the rights of the Church. Most significantly, he also swore that he would 'restore the good laws of his ancestors and especially the laws of King Edward (the Confessor), eradicating bad laws, and that he would judge all his men according to the just judgement of his court, restoring right to each and everybody'.[10] Here, in embryo, we have the basis for what was later to be negotiated, in detail, at Runnymede.

John had originally intended to launch his campaign against France in 1213. The time was ripe. Barrels of silver bought allies and troops. In the south, Aragon and Toulouse mustered a great army. In the north, France was confronted by the German Empire, by Flanders and Boulogne. But John was obliged to delay his campaign, first by Philip's own invasion threat, then for his negotiations with the Pope. When that July the English barons were eventually summoned for service overseas, too few attended the muster. There was a particularly ominous absence of knights or barons from Yorkshire and the north. John was obliged to write to Count Raymond of Toulouse, explaining that 'a great quantity of wind in England' had delayed his sailing.[11] The wind here was more figurative than meteorological: the consequence of the barons' reluctance either to serve John in southern France or to lend aid to the Count of Toulouse, a reputed heretic. It was in part as a result of this reluctance that, in September 1213, Raymond was defeated and King Pedro of Aragon killed at the Battle of Muret outside Toulouse. Raymond and his son, John's kinsmen, fled to England. To most people these were the king's remote colonial concerns. But as John himself must have realized, Muret dealt a crushing blow to the coalition planning to attack France from both the south and north. As a result, John was obliged to divide his own invasion force.

In February 1214, leaving England in the care of Peter des Roches, his French-born Bishop of Winchester, John set sail for La Rochelle. From here he would campaign on the southern frontiers of France. A second English army, commanded by William Longsword, was transported to Flanders, joining Otto of Brunswick to attack King Philip from the north. This was the most complex international military operation mounted from England since Richard I's crusade of the early 1190s. Philip was about to be caught in the jaws of a well-sprung trap. Or so it was hoped.

What if John had died in 1214, killed in a hunting accident or drowned on his crossing to La Rochelle? What would posterity have made of him? Would he be remembered today merely as 'John the unlucky' or as 'John the victim of circumstance'? Perhaps. But surely enough has already been reported here to suggest that John's successes would always have been outweighed by his failures. Even had he defeated the French and won back his lost lands, the cost, both financial and political, would have been enormous, provoked entirely by John's earlier defeats. His successes at Mirebeau and Carrickfergus were squandered in acts of brutality that disgusted his enemies and won him no friends. Though worse was still to come, John's regime was already doomed to infamy. It is to the personality behind that regime that we must now turn. What, we must ask, was wrong with John?

4
The Worst of All Our Kings
Tyranny Unmasked?

Combining the tastes of Caligula with the morals of an absconding bookmaker, King John is popularly perceived as a monster: in the words of William Stubbs, 'the very worst of all our kings', worse even than the notorious tyrants Edward II, Richard II or Richard III. Even if we ignore the Victorian varnish later applied here, this portrait is an ancient one. Within only a few years of John's death, Matthew Paris, chronicler of St Albans Abbey, was proclaiming: 'Foul as is Hell, John's presence there makes it fouler still!'[1] We search the chroniclers in vain for any even remotely favourable opinion of John. True, a northern Frenchman, familiar with John's court, declared that 'he spent lavishly; he gave plenty to eat, and did so generously and willingly'. But this only in qualification of a wider judgement that John was

a very bad man, more cruel than all others. He lusted after beautiful women, and because of this he shamed the high men of the land, for which reason he was greatly hated. Whenever he could, he told lies rather than the truth. He set his barons against one another whenever he could; he was very happy when he saw hate between them. He hated and was jealous of all honourable men; it greatly displeased him when he saw anyone acting well. He was brim-full of evil qualities.[2]

Here we have the very acme of tyranny, a concept attributed by the king's contemporaries to rulers who pursued their own selfish interests – territorial, sexual, financial – at the expense of public or communal need. Those writing of tyranny had no shortage of models upon which to draw. In this way, John, like his father before him, was regularly likened to the blackest of villains from the classical or biblical pasts: to Pharaoh, to Herod, or to the Roman emperors whose deeds were chronicled by Suetonius, still our chief source for Roman imperial misbehaviour.

Some, as early as the 1190s, may have looked to Suetonius' portrait of the emperor Domitian, younger brother of the heroic Titus who was himself identified with Richard I. Richard, like Titus, was a would-be conqueror of Jerusalem, while John, like Domitian, condemned his realm to murderous paranoia. In a similar vein, the French chronicler Guillaume le Breton deliberately compared John to Nero, another archetypal monster. Guillaume, indeed, paints an unforgettable scene of the murder of the terrified Arthur of Brittany, by night and in shadow, on board ship on the River Seine. Here John is reported to have plunged his sword twice, up to the hilt, into Arthur's brain and bowels, the lifeless corpse then drifting away on the tide: 'Behold, a deed worthy of Nero!' exclaims Guillaume. 'Behold a new Judas, a second Herod.'[3] Terrified innocence, copious bloodshed and the disposal of the victim's body by water were all standard themes in the lives of medieval child martyrs.

Even where the contemporary comparisons appear less black, on closer inspection their archetypes are no less villainous. To modern audiences, Nimrod, the mighty Old Testament huntsman, is a figure stirringly evoked in the music of Elgar. To those who knew their Bible, however, Nimrod was no less a tyrant than Belshazzar or Nebuchadnezzar. For the chroniclers to praise John as a mighty huntsman was therefore a distinctly two-edged compliment. Likewise, the so-called 'Barnwell annalist', more recently identified as a chronicler writing at Crowland Abbey in the Lincolnshire Fens, remarks that John resembled Marius, a Roman official of mixed fortunes, sometimes up and sometimes down. Modern commentators who cite this passage have failed to notice its bitterness. It is the Roman poet Lucan that the chronicler is citing here, and according to Lucan, Gaius Marius, the corrupt consul who first turned the legions against the people, stained the very steps of the Senate with the blood of civil war. As any reader of Lucan would know – and what educated person in John's reign had not read Lucan? – Marius's wars led directly to the Caesars, to empire and to Lucan's own patron, the emperor Nero. The analogy between King John and Nero thus hovered in the mind of the Crowland chronicler almost as vividly as in that of Guillaume le Breton.[4]

Some contemporaries risked direct judgements on John, rather than dressing their disapproval in classical or biblical metaphors. Such judgements were no less harsh. The biographer of William Marshal, for example, writing in the 1220s, in French, attempted what we might recognize as an early exercise in psychological profiling. Here we find John skulking through the back lanes of Normandy in 1203, rather than risk open confrontation with the French. What more could be expected, the writer asks, when 'a man who does not know whom he has to fear and who always thinks he is in an inferior position is bound to fear everybody'?[5]

Here we are also informed of John's lack of sense (*saveir*), his arrogance (*orgels*), and his sneering (*despleisante*) nature. Above all, the John we encounter is the resentful and generally despised younger son, the 'Lackland' or 'Softsword' reported by other chroniclers; in the words of the Marshal's biographer, the 'king without heritage' who those with memories of the 1170s or 1180s still recalled as a nobody, mocked even by his father.[6]

Others told stories that depended on inference rather than direct attack. The Irish annals, for example, tell us that in Ireland, in 1210, when asked to surrender his sons as hostages, the King of Connacht rode away from John's court and never returned.[7] The implication here was clear: John was not a man to be trusted with child hostages, even in the mind of an Irish brigand with only the vaguest notion of what might or might not have happened to Arthur of Brittany. The biographer of William Marshal makes a similar point, albeit in reverse, trumpeting the willingness of the Marshal to deliver up his sons as hostages, against the advice of his men.[8] Here, it is not so subtly suggested, was a baron so brave that he feared nobody, not even a paranoid slayer of innocent children.

The biography of the Marshal, like other contemporary narratives, credits John with a fair measure of wit. Certainly, if the chroniclers are to be believed, he was capable of both sarcasm and menace. In one such story, having enjoyed the hospitality of Archbishop Hubert Walter, John enquired of his host: 'Why have I stayed with you so long?' The archbishop replied that he assumed it was to do him honour. 'By God's teeth,' the king replied, 'it is not so.' How else, he asked, could he bankrupt a courtier who otherwise threatened to outdo him in magnificence? The chronicler allows John's victim a reply. Far from being terrified, the archbishop vowed to entertain John at the coming feast of Easter, and again at Pentecost, and still to remain a better man than his king.[9] Something similar is reported of Isabella of Angoulême, John's queen. Furious at the loss of his continental lands, John is said to have rounded on Isabella, demanding, 'Do you hear, my lady, all that I have lost for you?' Like Archbishop Hubert, Isabella replied in kind, telling her husband, in a witticism derived from the game of chess, that she had already lost the best knight in the world (Hugh de Lusignan), and that if John were not careful he would end up as 'a king (check-)mated in a corner'.[10] A contemporary romance reports that a great vendetta between King John and his childhood friend Fulk fitz Warin began when John, never a good loser, struck Fulk an almighty blow with the chessboard on which they had been playing.[11]

None of these stories is literal truth. All circulated only after John's death. All, none the less, suggest what

contemporaries thought *might* be believed. Like all anec-
dotes told at the expense of the powerful, plausibility
was their essential prerequisite. Modern writers who
attempt to defend John, presenting him as the victim of
posthumous slander, rather miss this point. True, many
of the more hair-raising stories of the king's iniquity
emerged only after his death. But the fact that these stories were believed and widely circulated, as with similar
tales told of Stalin or Nixon or Mao, suggests their inherent
verisimilitude.

Here, the chroniclers of St Albans overreached themselves, wielding not so much the rapier as the bludgeon.
John, they alleged, was a sadist, lecher and would-be apos-
tate: a demon in all but outward form. According to Roger
of Wendover (d. *c.*1236), first of the great St Albans historians, John lost Normandy in 1203 because he was too busy
dallying with his young bride, refusing to rise from his bed
to fight the French. According to Wendover's successor and
reviser, Matthew Paris (*c.*1200–1259), when John entered
into negotiations with the King of Morocco, even going so
far as to offer to convert to Islam, his ambassador was
asked for a true account of the king's morals. John, the
ambassador reported, was a tyrant, a seducer of the pubes-
cent daughters and sisters of his barons. Far from
responding to his embraces, his wife hated him with a pas-
sion. Frequently convicted of incest and sorcery, she was
condemned to watch her many adulterous lovers strangled
to death in her own bed.[12]

Both Wendover and Paris repeat the story of Geoffrey,
'Archdeacon of Norwich'. An Exchequer official, supposedly

overheard making disparaging remarks about the king, Geoffrey was arrested, tortured and put to death at John's command, crushed under the weight of a cope constructed from lead. In reality, and contrary to this account, the Geoffrey in question was not an archdeacon but an official placed over the Jews. He none the less disappeared in 1212, at the same time that John unmasked conspiracy among other members of his court.[13] Like the starving to death of Matilda de Braose, Geoffrey's fate remains a matter of hearsay, albeit of hearsay that contemporaries had little difficulty in believing.

How are we to assess the degree of exaggeration here? How, after more than eight hundred years, can we hope to discover whether John was truly as black as the chroniclers painted him? A partial answer is supplied from the records of John's own writing office, the so-called 'chancery rolls' (scrolled-up parchment sheets on which the king's clerks kept copies of a large proportion of his outgoing letters). Divided into distinct categories, of 'Charter', 'Patent' or 'Close' rolls, according to the particular type of letter they record, year by year these preserve many thousands of written instruments. Every time, for example, that the king wished one of his local officers, a sheriff or a constable, to carry out a particular command, this might involve the issue of up to half a dozen royal letters. Every time that money was disbursed, either from the central Exchequer or locally, this might be authorized in writing issued in the king's name. Gathered into their series, the rolls were then carefully preserved. By May 1215, they had their own keeper, addressed by the king as William

'Cuckoo Well', perhaps named after his function as an echoer of past business.[14] William was the first in a distinguished line of such 'Masters of the Rolls' stretching forwards to the present day.

The survival of so great a quantity of rolled-up parchment can itself be read as evidence of John's paranoia. Why else have all of these records made and kept unless John was a control freak, determined to keep an eye on every aspect of what to his predecessors had appeared dull routine? In reality, the rolls testify more to prudence than to paranoia. At a time when both England and France were gearing up for war, it made perfect sense for John to preserve records that directly affected income and expenditure. On a lesser scale, the chancery of King Philip of France attempted something similar, preserving Philip's letters albeit more selectively and in books rather than rolls. By most modern historians, the chancery rolls are cited as evidence of the king's competence rather than his wickedness, indeed by some historians as evidence of John's 'administrative genius'.[15]

Certainly, a great number of the letters preserved in these rolls testify to administrative routine. Even so, because the rolls were the king's private resource and not yet an official 'public record', they can be surprisingly indiscreet. Here, more or less wherever we turn, we find evidence that does not so much contradict as confirm the accepted picture of John's villainy. The king was no fool. He committed few if any of his darker secrets to writing. After Mirebeau or Carrickfergus, for example, we find no letters commanding the murder of Arthur of Brittany or the starvation of

1. John (bottom left), his father Henry II, his elder brother Richard I (with sword) and his son and successor Henry III (bottom right), as depicted by the chronicler Matthew Paris c. 1240. Note the crown slipping from John's head.

2. John as depicted in the fourteenth century, a mighty huntsman, but pursuing a sport itself often synonymous with violence and tyranny.

3. John's great seal, front and back, our only contemporary portrait of him. Note the role of the king in dispensing justice and in vigorously defending his realm. In neither function was John to distinguish himself.

4. Angers on the Loire, cradle of the Angevin dynasty, yet one of the great cities of northern France that John was to abandon in 1204 and thereafter to strive unsuccessfully to recover.

5. Arthur, John's young nephew, here shown proudly displaying his titles as ruler not only of Brittany but of Aquitaine, bestowed on him by the French king in a deliberate challenge to John.

6. A digital reconstruction of Dublin Castle. John first came to maturity in Ireland, where the harsh realities of colonial rule were to impact upon his later rule as king. Note here the vast stone fortress and walls (much still extant), built using the slave labour of the colonized.

7. Queen Isabella, John's second wife, heiress to the southern French county of Angoulême. In marrying her, John provoked rebellion by the lords of Poitou, in due course leagued with King Philip of France.

8. Corfe Castle in Dorset. Here various of John's state prisoners are reputed to have been brutally mistreated. The castle itself was ruined in the seventeenth century, in the later English Civil War.

9. The seal of Stephen Langton, Archbishop of Canterbury, front and back. Langton's exclusion from England by King John resulted in papal interdict. Thereafter, it was Langton who helped co-ordinate opposition to the king by Church and barons. Note the image of Becket's martyrdom on the back of his seal, with the hand of God reaching down.

10. One of the consequences of papal interdict as depicted by Matthew Paris: all church bells to be silenced.

11. Carrickfergus Castle, in 1210 skilfully besieged and captured by John whose subsequent mishandling of his prisoners provoked yet further baronial outrage and defection.

12. Runnymede, with Windsor Castle in the distance. Chosen as a site lying between London and the king, on the border between four English shires and four bishoprics.

13. The Articles of the Barons (c. May–June 1215): the draft peace agreement by which John agreed terms with the rebel barons.

14. Magna Carta: one of the four surviving originals of the charter sealed at Runnymede. Note the additional clauses inserted in the lower margin.

15. John's tomb (c. 1230) at Worcester Cathedral, flanked by Saints Oswald and Wulfstan. Note that the king's sword bends as its point enters the lion's mouth.

Matilda de Braose. What we do have, none the less, is a letter of August 1202 concerning the prisoners captured on the same occasion as Arthur. This letter survives because the king had deliberately restricted access to his prisoners, but had then, in ways all too familiar today, forgotten the passwords he himself had set. Today we might be obliged to call up our internet provider. John simply blustered, commanding the constable of Falaise to allow his representative access to Geoffrey de Lusignan, one of his state prisoners, even though 'we do not well recollect' what 'countersign' had been agreed. Should discussions over Geoffrey's ransom go according to plan, then the constable was to release Geoffrey from his fetters and 'put him in the place where the ring-chains are'.[16] Casual references to ring-chains, fetters and the incarceration of state prisoners speak of a regime habitually accustomed to both secrecy and brutality.

Besides cruelty, the king was regularly accused of lechery. Once again, we should not expect John to confess his sins in writing. He undoubtedly fathered several bastards, but all of these might have been born before his first marriage, in 1189. It was from one of his illegitimate daughters, Joan, the wife of the Welsh prince Llewelyn, that John is said first to have heard rumours of the assassination plot in 1212.[17] Various reports that have been read in the past as referring to royal mistresses might be supplied with more innocent explanations. Take, for example, a reference in the king's household accounts for 1212. Here we find a servant of the French-born Philip Marc, Sheriff of Nottingham, reimbursed two shillings for a chaplet of roses that he carried from the king to the king's 'lady friend'. But when precisely did a 'lady friend' become a mistress, and was this particular 'lady friend' a mistress or perhaps merely the king's wife or daughter?[18]

Here too we must look for casual rather than precise corroboration. We find it, soon enough, in references that suggest an unchivalrous, indeed a predatory approach to women. Some of these references remain elusive. Peter des Roches, French-born Bishop of Winchester, for example, was once fined a barrel of good wine 'for failing to remind the king about a belt for the countess of Aumale'.[19] The wife of the king's chief forester, Hugh de Neville, offered John two hundred chickens 'so that she might lie one night with her husband'.[20] Was this, as some historians have proposed, an attempt by Hugh's wife to escape from her duties as the king's mistress, or was it a joking reference to the ways in which royal duties had deprived her of her husband's company? In either case, the fact that Hugh's wife, and both of John's queens, Isabella of Gloucester and Isabella of Angoulême, were lodged for extended periods in Hugh's castle at Marlborough must have led to potentially embarrassing encounters.

In the autumn of 1214, the king sent Isabella of Angoulême into safe keeping at Berkhamsted. Shortly afterwards, he despatched a letter to the constable there that on the surface appears entirely anodyne and in which he writes:

Know that, by God's grace, we are in good health and unharmed, and we order you to restore, as soon as you can, the horse that you borrowed from Richard the Fleming. We shall shortly be coming to your part of the country, and we shall be thinking of you, about the hawk, and though it might be ten years since we last saw you, at our coming it shall seem to us no more than three days. Take good care of the charge that we have entrusted to you, letting us know regularly of the condition of this charge.[21]

The 'charge' here can almost certainly be identified as the queen and her infant children, so that what we have, in effect, is a coded reference to Isabella, combined with a reminder, menacing or amorous as we choose to interpret it, that the king had his eye on her and her keepers. If Isabella herself was the 'hawk' referred to earlier in the letter, then we would have to ask what sort of husband refers to his wife as a bird of prey. The king certainly kept a close eye on his hawks. In March 1215, for example, he wrote to John fitz Hugh, constable of Windsor. Commanded to receive four hawks, one of them described as the king's best gyrfalcon, fitz Hugh was given detailed instructions on what to feed these birds: 'fat goats', 'good' chickens, and the meat of hares at least once a week. To ensure the birds' safety, he was to seek out the best mastiffs as guard dogs.[22] According to contemporary falconry manuals, where emperors might hunt with eagles, gyrfalcons from Norway were reserved for kings. As the most prestigious of raptors, they were to be flown against the largest and most aggressive of prey. In particular this involved attacks against cranes and herons, both of which are capable of putting up the stiffest defence. The king took pleasure in such shows, just as elsewhere in watching duels between accused felons. In 1212, for example, he fed fifty paupers in penance for each of the seven cranes that he had hunted on Holy Innocents' Day (28 December).[23] What sort of ruler, we might ask, chooses to watch the most blood-thirsty of animal slaughter on a day otherwise pledged to commemoration of the children massacred by Herod? Not just this, but on the eve of 29 December, the feast most solemnly dedicated to the memory of Thomas Becket, victim of the most notorious act of bloodshed ever committed by John's notoriously violent family?

There are further insights to be obtained from King John's hunting of cranes. Clerks in the royal chancery had long been accustomed to doodling or inserting informal comments in the margins of official records. Just such a doodle is to be found in the left-hand margin of one of John's chancery rolls next to letters of the king dated August 1216. This shows a large bird, the name 'Philippa of Paulton' and a rhyming Latin couplet, referring to 'a mad crane'.[24] What was intended was probably a carica-ture of a woman, named Philippa of Paulton, depicted here in the guise of a bird famous both for its size and its distinc-tively plaintive cry. She may have attended court to plead for her kinsman Roger of Paulton, one-time deputy sheriff of Somerset. The caricature of her is no masterpiece. Even so, it reveals a royal clerk, bored and doodling, mocking as a 'mad crane' a woman who, for all we know, had good cause to lament the king's hawk-like ruthlessness. This was a court that delighted in the victimization not just of animals but of its human supplicants, and most particularly of women.

Rumour suggests that John seduced not merely low-born courtesans but the wives and daughters of his barons. We struggle to find precise proof here. A century or more later, it was alleged that the daughter of Robert fitz Walter, 'the fair Matilda', had suffered death by poison for refusing the king's advances. Later still, this same strand of heavily mythologized storytelling contributed to the Victorian legends of Maid Marian, lover of the even more mythical Robin Hood.[25] But some such stories dated from within only a few years of John's death. According to a French (and therefore heavily biased) report, when the king's half-brother William Longsword, Earl of Salisbury, was imprisoned in France in 1214, John seized the opportunity to seduce William's wife.[26] Of the other barons implicated in rebellion, Eustace de Vescy, it was later alleged, had only narrowly escaped being cuckolded by the king. In a story rich in classical resonances, the king is said to have been tricked, finding 'a hideous whoring washerwoman' introduced to his bed instead of Eustace's wife.[27]

Given the infidelities of his ancestors, there was nothing unusual about John's affairs. None of the accusations against him has been proved. By contrast, King Henry I maintained an entire harem of well-born mistresses on his manors around Oxford, fathering so many bastards that, even today, historians dispute their number. Henry II seems to have seduced not only the wife of one of his barons but the same man's daughter and niece. From one of these adulterous encounters William Longsword was born.[28] For doing what his father and great-grandfather had done with impunity, however, John provoked not merely censure but armed resistance. In part, this reflects a change in aristocratic sensibilities, in accordance with the Church's increasingly sacramentalized attitude to marriage vows. In part, we find John yet again struggling to inspire even the reluctant awe accorded to his ancestors.

The Church was influential here in highlighting the king's more general impiety. John was not without respect for the Church. He founded a Cistercian abbey, at Faringdon in Berkshire (now Oxfordshire), later moved to Beaulieu on Southampton Water. He confirmed and occasionally augmented his ancestors' grants to monasteries and cathedrals. In the eyes of monastic chroniclers, however, long familiar with the legends of Thomas Becket, John's essentially political struggles with the papacy and Archbishop Langton rendered him little short of an infidel. A would-be convert to Islam who never properly attended Mass, John, it was claimed, not only allied himself to the heretics of Toulouse but trusted to magic and totems, including the jewel, hung around his neck, that he believed would protect him from defeat. Such stories are surely mere fables, invented by churchmen piqued by the king's refusal to be governed by popes or bishops. Or are they? A royal letter of November 1201, for example, reveals John rewarding a man named Bartholomew of Berkhamsted, finder of 'the precious stones and jewels that we used to wear around our neck'.[29] Another such stone, believed to render its owner invincible in battle, is said to have been kept in the royal treasury until treasonably handed over to the Welsh, in the reign of John's son, Henry III.[30]

For John's delight in jewels we can turn to lists, preserved in the chancery rolls. In June 1215, for example, a
week after Magna Carta, we find the king acknowledging
receipt of a great quantity of precious objects, silver and
ebony boxes containing relics of the saints, and 'a gold
vase with the pearls that the lord Pope sent us'.[31] Papal
gifts, from peacock crowns to pearls, were clearly prized
at court. So too were such treasures as the sword of the
legendary hero Tristan, carried to court for the Christmas
festivities of 1207.[32] So too were books. For what we know
of the king's library we depend on lists of things consigned
to safe keeping, often to the royal abbey at Reading in
Berkshire. In March 1208, for example, we find John in
Sussex, receiving more than a dozen books from Reading.
These included the predictable (an Old Testament), the
theological (Origen of Alexandria, Saint Augustine, Hugh
of Saint-Victor, Peter the Lombard's *Sentences*) and the
downright esoteric (Candidus Arianus, *On the Divine Generation*, a rare book even in monastic hands).[33] Quite why
they were produced at court at this particular moment
remains unclear, but it is worth noting that the king's sudden
interest in theology coincided with the imposition of the
papal interdict on 24 March. Preparing to enter a battle of
words with the Church, it was perhaps wise for John and his
supporters to arm themselves with the most learned of
authorities ancient and modern.

Whether this proves any real literacy on the king's behalf
remains uncertain. John's early upbringing at Fontevraud
might suggest an intended clerical career and hence a train-
ing in both reading and writing. In later life, besides possessing

books, including histories of his ancestors, John cracked jokes that savour of the schoolroom rather than the stables. In April 1215, for example, a royal letter to the Pope not only indulged in learned banter about Isaiah, Moses and the 'bean-eaters' mocked by St Jerome, but used, for the first time in any discourse attributed to a French-speaking king, a phrase in English, referring to the 'seven churches' (*sevnchurch*) instructed by Saint Paul. This only a few weeks after the chancery rolls preserve the very first official royal letter to survive written in French.[34] Appropriately enough, John's French correspondence, of January 1215, concerns negotiations with Archbishop Langton over Rochester Castle, attempting to wriggle out of arrangements that neither the king nor the archbishop could entirely trust, and therefore best dealt with in the informality of written French rather than in the firmer legal certainties of Latin.

Those who collect jewels, relics and books often cite utility or good taste to mask their kleptomania. Yet kleptomania itself shades all too easily into pleonexia: the insatiable urge to possess things that rightfully belong to others, whether property, wives or reputation. John's court was a place of generous hospitality where courtiers competed to display their spending power. There was none the less a sinister side to such displays. To begin with, there was the king's fickle humour. Flemish mercenaries, expecting to be paid at Marlborough in 1215, watched in disgust as a great quantity of treasure was piled up before the king. From this John refused to disburse a single penny.[35] Hand in hand with this went John's tendency to exploit the bravado expected of the great. Why else, save to compete in such bravado, did William de Braose offer the king the absurd sum of 40,000 marks in settlement of his debts? What else can have induced Hubert Walter to boast of bankrupting himself in entertaining the king? Many of the more notorious of John's financial transactions can be explained in these terms, not so much as fines arbitrarily imposed, but as the result of competition between barons outdoing one another in the extravagance of their wagers. Once again we might note that this was a time when the super-rich were becoming significantly richer. In an age of oligarchs, boastful vulgarity trumps most other forms of statesmanship. Indeed, the state itself becomes the plaything of the newly wealthy.

Take, for example, a deal almost as notorious as that struck with William de Braose. Before the king sailed to France in 1214, Geoffrey de Mandeville, Earl of Essex, offered 20,000 marks to marry Isabella of Gloucester, the king's first wife, divorced and in royal keeping for the past fifteen years. In putting his former bride up for sale, the king accepted an offer that both he and Geoffrey must have known to be absurd. Isabella was at least fifty years old. She had no prospect of childbearing and her more valuable estates had long ago been plundered. Geoffrey failed to meet even the first instalment of his debt. As a result, like William de Braose before him, he placed himself entirely at the mercy of a notoriously unmerciful king. What we have here, surely, is the one-upmanship of the super-rich. Similar extravagances might be found in ancient Rome, in the gentlemen's clubs of eighteenth-century London, or indeed amid the oligarchs of present-day Moscow or Shanghai. What distinguished John's court was the presence of a king happy to pour the wine and to watch the play, but happier still to pounce, like a village usurer, whenever a gambler strayed beyond his reasonable ability to pay.

When rebellion came, it was, as remarked by J. C. Holt, 'a rebellion of the King's debtors'.[36] It was also, in many instances, a rebellion of the king's former friends. John's friendships were notoriously fickle. In 1199, on becoming king, he had cold-shouldered many of those who had served him during his time as count of Mortain. Thereafter, no one approaching his court could be entirely sure whether he would be embraced or embezzled. The chronicler Roger of Wendover supplies us with a list of thirty-two men whom he labels John's 'most evil counsellors', men who had urged the King 'not towards reason but towards [arbitrary] will'.[37] Most of these men were born in the 1160s or 1170s and were therefore John's contemporaries: an interesting feature of John's inner circle that set his court apart from that of other kings who had encouraged a more diverse mingling of generations. Of the thirty-two men listed by Wendover, several were already dead by the time that rebellion broke out in 1215. However, at least eleven of the others rebelled, in five cases unequivocally before the king's death.

Some of these rebellious 'friends' sprang from well-established courtier dynasties, a constituency that then as now has tended to be most vociferous in its criticism of royal misbehaviour. Reginald of Cornhill, son and successor to Henry II's Sheriff of Kent, Hugh de Neville, grandson of Henry II's chief forester, or Gilbert fitz Reinfrey, Sheriff of Lancashire and nephew of Henry II's chancellor, were all second- or third-generation courtiers conditioned to nostalgia for the good old days. But others, such as the chief administrator of estates confiscated during the papal interdict, John fitz Hugh, or the chief organizer of John's naval forces, William of Wrotham, had no such family tradition behind them. On the contrary, these were men who owed everything to John yet who none the less betrayed him either for personal gain or the public good.

There were as many motives here as there were individual rebels. So let us examine a particular case. We have already found Hugh de Neville, the king's chief forester, as a party to the joking fine over chickens wagered by his wife. Several years later, turning a blind eye to the activities of another royal favourite, Hugh permitted Peter des Roches, Bishop of Winchester, to set aside a hunting park at Taunton on land that was allegedly part of the royal forest. For this, Hugh was fined 1,000 marks. Bishop Peter on the other hand, far from being punished, was granted deer by the king with which to stock his new park. In the same year, 1210, Hugh was granted custody of prisoners captured at Carrickfergus. Two of these men escaped. For this, Hugh was fined a further 6,000 marks (£4,000).[38] Little if any of this money was ever collected. If questioned, the king might have shrugged it off as joshing between friends. No prudent ruler, however, provokes his subordinates merely to raise a laugh.

'Laughing', or perhaps more accurately 'sneering', is one of the adjectives that contemporaries most regularly applied to John. We find it used as early as 1185, to describe John's taunting of the native Irish. It was there again in 1199, in the mocked solemnities of John's inauguration as Duke of

Normandy. When the wine flowed and the king wanted sport, the court itself could become a theatre of cruelty. Philippa of Paulton or the wife of Hugh de Neville knew this. So did the king's half-brother Geoffrey Plantagenet, Archbishop of York. Falling at John's feet to beg for favour, the archbishop was obliged to watch as the king, 'laughing', threw himself to the ground. The word 'laughing' is once again significant here. 'See, my lord archbishop,' the king declared, 'I have done for you just as much as you have for me!'[39]

This was not a king whose promises could be believed. Quick to collect his winnings, reluctant ever to honour his debts, John undermined all trust. At the same time, he began to demand ever more extravagant assurances of loyalty from those around him. Hostages and monetary pledges no longer sufficed. In 1205, and again in 1209, he commanded that the entire adult population of England swear him oaths of fealty, presumably as protection against the threat that the King of France or the Pope might seek to depose him. In 1205, and again in 1213, when invasion seemed imminent, those failing to assist the defence of the realm were threatened with perpetual disinheritance and 'culvertage' – the legal process whereby freemen were debased to the status of serfs or slaves.[40] In 1213, William Marshal and twenty-six Irish landowners were persuaded to issue a written declaration of support for the king. Here they stated specifically that John, to their knowledge, had maintained faith with them and committed no offence 'against the constitutions of his realm or against his faithful men'.[41] A few months later, twelve English earls and barons, taking oaths on the Gospels, were persuaded to guarantee the settlement that John had reached with the Church.[42] In 1214, we find two members of John's body-guard bound by oath to the king to report anything that they might hear spoken against him: in effect, the origin of the privy councillor's oath still sworn today.[43] Oaths and formal pledges now usurped the place previously occupied by trust. The problem remained: trust is a commodity denied to those themselves deemed untrustworthy. As John and his barons were about to discover, not even the most sol-emn oaths could bind a perjurer.

5
The Reckoning at Runnymede

Having waited eight long years to launch reconquest, in February 1214, as we saw at the end of Chapter 3, John crossed to France, disembarking at La Rochelle. His campaign prospered. In March and April, he reimposed his authority over the region between the rivers Loire and Garonne. At La Réole on the Garonne, his troops confronted and forced the withdrawal of the crusading army led by Simon de Montfort. John's priority thereafter was to reassert his authority north and east of La Rochelle. Here the Lusignan family had stepped into the vacuum created by John's expulsion from France after 1204. Again, all went well. Lusignan castles were besieged and captured; the Lusignans themselves were bought off with a settlement that promised marriage to one of the king's daughters and a major assignment of reconquered land in Poitou or elsewhere. By early June, John was ready to press home his attack against the chief centres of French royal influence, north of the Loire. In early June, he laid siege to Nantes, failing to take the city but on a nearby bridge capturing Robert of Dreux, a cousin of the King of France. On 17 June, moving eastwards along the Loire, John entered the city of Angers, his family's ancestral home. He had visited

Angers before, during his expedition of 1206. Indeed, it is possible that between 1204 and 1214 he was a more frequent visitor to the city than its new titular overlord, the King of France. From Angers, on 19 June, he set out to besiege the fortress of La Roche-aux-Moines on the Loire's north bank.

The castle of La Roche-aux-Moines is today a ruin set within an estate producing white wine. Had John's siege gone differently, it might today be commemorated as the site of an English victory as famous as Blenheim or Waterloo. Instead, John again proved that discretion was no substitute for valour. On the Loire, he had been met with delegations from Normandy, apparently seeking to negotiate a return to Plantagenet allegiance. After the French conquest of 1204, the Normans had never been fully reconciled to French rule. Norman landowners, not least cathedrals and monasteries, had been dependent on resources in England and considered themselves impoverished by the French conquest. Churches fell into disrepair; land, influence and offices were conferred on the French king's cronies. By June 1214, with Philip of France too heavily engaged against John's German and Flemish allies to send anything but a token force under his son, Louis, to oppose John on the Loire, an English reconquest of Normandy seemed possible. But offered an opportunity at La Roche for a decisive engagement, John once again chose to flee, perhaps alarmed by rumours of treachery among his own French allies. He thereby saved his skin at the cost of what many considered rank cowardice. As in 1204, his possessions were simply abandoned to the French, amid accusations of treason and betrayal. Worse still, having retreated south across the Loire on or around 2 July, by early August the king began to hear rumours of an even worse defeat in the north. On Sunday 27 July, at Bouvines outside Lille, King Philip of France had annihilated John's allies from Flanders and the German Empire. A large part of the English expeditionary force had been either killed or captured.

The road from Bouvines to Runnymede was both short and straight. Already, even before Bouvines, John had faced hostility or indifference from a number of English barons. Eighteen of the twenty-five barons later leagued together at Runnymede had failed either to serve in person or to send knights to represent them in John's army in Poitou. Many more now resisted the payment of scutage. Although a five-year truce with the French was agreed in mid September 1214, John now had other enemies with whom to contend. Besides the restless English baronage, there was the Church, still demanding compensation for injuries suffered during the papal interdict. Although most of the bishops were likely to remain loyal to the king, Giles de Braose, Bishop of Hereford, was rumoured to be in open alliance with the Welsh. In the far north, there was the perennial prospect of trouble from the Scots. In Gascony and the far south, in 1214 as after 1204, there was the risk of an attack either by Simon de Montfort or the King of Castile.

In 1212, John had responded to threats of rebellion and deposition with appeasement. He now attempted something similar. However, his chief assets were already spent. Earlier promises of reform had not been kept. Of the 100,000 marks pledged in compensation to the Church, less than 40,000 had actually been paid. As a substitute, the king made a series of extravagant awards, offering Rochester Castle to the Archbishop of Canterbury, Glastonbury Abbey to the Bishop of Bath, other lands to the Bishops of Ely, Lincoln and Worcester, as alternatives to cash. This process culminated, on 21 November 1214, with a new royal charter. Where previously the king had controlled the election of his own favourites as bishops or abbots, he would now permit 'free' election on the part of the English Church, subject only to royal licence and the exclusion of candidates totally obnoxious to John or his successors.

Such promises were a substitute for anything more concrete because the king's great treasure, painstakingly collected in taxes and exactions over the past decade, had been squandered on war in France. But could such promises be trusted? At precisely the same time that he was offering free elections, John was engaged in attempts to preserve the bishoprics of Durham, Rochester and York and the abbeys of St Albans and Bury St Edmunds against freely elected candidates of whom he disapproved. A royal crony, Richard Marsh, travelled from monastery to monastery securing written undertakings from the monks to forego all financial compensation owed from the time of the papal interdict. Marsh, chiefly known for a love of beer, was in due course made both royal chancellor and Bishop of Durham. Between John's promises and what he did in practice a great gulf still loomed.

For the third time in less than a dozen years, John had slunk back to England impoverished and defeated. The

Anglo-French truce of September had been witnessed by no fewer than twenty-one English barons. Of these, two (Walter de Lacy and Fulk fitz Warin) were already former rebels, and a further four were leaders of the rebellion that, in the autumn of 1214, was about to catch fire.

The emergence of the baronial coalition that drove the rebellion against John remains difficult to trace, being necessarily hidden from the king and the clerks who compiled our principal sources of information, the records of the royal chancery. We must depend instead upon hints and glimpses. Beyond doubt, resistance to scutage now became a symbol of rebel solidarity. The administration of John's tax collapsed in the face of widespread refusal to pay.

To fend off the threat from the Welsh, and to demonstrate his continued strength in the Welsh Marches, John staged his Christmas feast in the west Midlands city of Worcester, a location never before employed for such festivities. He did not stay long. After the great hymn of rulership the 'Laudes' ('Christ has conquered, Christ reigns') was sung, and a feast at which at least fifty deer and sixty pigs were consumed by his court, John hurried back to London. There, on neutral ground belonging to the Templars, between the Thames and the Strand, within the precinct of the modern Inns of Court, a great council was held. It lasted almost a week. The chronicler Roger of Wendover tells us that, in November 1214, various baronial malcontents had already met at Bury St Edmunds, swearing to make war on the king should he refuse their demands. The precise details here, as with Archbishop Langton's supposed rediscovery of the coronation charter of Henry I as a basis for good law to be imposed on King John, have been much debated. What is unquestionable is that by the time of the London conference of January 1215 it was clear to the king that a baronial conspiracy had emerged and that he would henceforth be obliged either to negotiate with his opponents, or to destroy them. The term 'Northerners' was now first applied to the malcontents. As perhaps the first use in English history of a party-political label, this term, the 'Northerners', now came to signify a group brought together by common political ambitions rather than by mere kinship or personal loyalty.[1]

Both sides, king and barons, despatched embassies to the Pope. From the records of these embassies we obtain our first clear evidence both of the identity of the leading conspirators – here named as the northern landowners Eustace de Vescy and Richard de Percy – and of the Pope's attempts to mediate a settlement, using Archbishop Langton and the English bishops as his go-betweens. As early as March 1215, papal letters recommended that the king refer all ongoing disputes to judgement 'by peers or by the law of the land', a phrase subsequently incorporated within clause 39 of Magna Carta as a key definition of the rule of law.

The stand-off between John and the barons continued through the early months of 1215. With negotiations postponed to 26 April, John used the time to build up his military strength and to seek papal support. The Pope was a passionate supporter of the planned crusade to rescue Jerusalem. On Ash Wednesday, 4 March 1215, John took crusading vows. As the campaigning season approached, both sides prepared their castles for war. The king raised mercenaries from France and Ireland. The barons sought support in Rome, and perhaps too at the court of King Philip in Paris. The meeting of 26 April went by default. Instead, over the next few days, upwards of fifty barons and their retinues assembled at Brackley, north of Oxford, one of the few locations in England where tournaments were regularly licensed and therefore a venue familiar to many who now gathered there in arms. On or around 27 April, the barons issued a written defiance of the king, appointing Robert fitz Walter and Geoffrey de Mandeville as their military commanders.

John himself was reluctant to acknowledge this declaration of civil war. His hand was forced, however, first by a failed baronial siege of Northampton, and then by the baronial seizure of London, on Sunday 17 May, supposedly by stealth through a secretly opened gate while leading citizens were at Mass. The Londoners had reasons of their own to join the rebellion, having suffered disproportionately both from royal taxation and from the repeated seizures of foreign ships intended to prevent the French from acquiring an invasion fleet.

With his capital city in enemy hands, the king retreated to Windsor. Runnymede, part way between London and Windsor, was chosen as the site of negotiations, to be brokered chiefly through the Church. A neutral location, Runnymede was neither entirely water-meadow nor dry land, lying on the Thames at the point of convergence between four English counties (Middlesex, Surrey, Berkshire and Buckinghamshire) and four ecclesiastical dioceses (London, Winchester, Salisbury and Lincoln).

What happened at Runnymede has been so often described that we risk ignoring a key detail. Although the debate between king and barons produced a series of written instruments intended to guarantee peace, this delayed but did not arrest the slide to war.

One of these written instruments, by 1217 already being described as 'the great charter' (in Latin 'Magna Carta', to distinguish it from a briefer instrument, issued later, dealing specifically with the law of the royal forests), set out in remarkable detail the concessions that King John was forced to make. In more than sixty clauses, king and barons thrashed out terms intended to put an end to the worst excesses of royal government, not only as practised under John but as experienced over more than fifty years of Plantagenet misrule.

More than half the clauses of Magna Carta concern matters in which John and his ancestors had abused the privileges of lordship that might be deemed either 'reasonable' or 'customary'. Thus there are clauses dealing with inheritance and wardship (clauses 2–5), marriage and widowhood (clauses 6–8), debt and its collection (clauses 9–11, 26–7, including debt owed to Jews), scutage and other taxes (clauses 12–13, 15), lordship over fees and churches (clauses 32, 46), service including that owed to the king's armies (clauses 16, 23, 28–31, 37, 43), the forests (clauses 44, 47–8, 53), the profits of justice (clauses 20–22), and the particular mercantile concerns of the City of London and other towns (clauses 13, 33, 35, 41–2). Other clauses are given over not so much to the principles as to the procedures of the law. Here, besides a general prohibition against arbitrary accusations (clause 38), judgements (clause 39) and the sale of justice (clause 40), there are clauses intended to protect the jurisdiction of baronial courts (clause 34), restricting the judicial powers of sheriffs (clause 24), and insisting that justice be made available speedily and at fixed times and locations (clause 17). For the rest, we find an eclectic mixture of principle and pragmatism. Thus clauses forbidding arbitrary judgement or the sale of justice (clauses 39–40) sit side by side with others intended to smooth relations with Wales and Scotland (clauses 56–9), or (in the case of clauses 50–51) to ensure the exile of the king's foreign mercenaries, specifically naming the 'alien' kinsmen of Girard d'Athée serving as constables or sheriffs at Windsor, Hereford, Bristol, Gloucester and Nottingham.

All this, astonishingly, the king was persuaded to accept. Yet how to ensure that his promises were kept? Here the charter skirted dangerously close to denying what both the king and the Pope would have regarded as John's God-given right to rule. Not only was no appeal to be allowed to any higher authority (meaning Pope Innocent), but the charter's final clauses entrusted its enforcement to twenty-five barons, authorized to make war on the king should he break any of the listed promises. County by county, knights were to swear oaths to the twenty-five and to lead inquiries into the worst excesses committed by the king and his officials. The twenty-five included no less than ten earls or eldest sons of earls. Even more remarkably, sixteen of the twenty-five were related, within only three or four degrees of kinship, both to Richard de Clare, Earl of Hertford, and to his cousin, Robert fitz Walter, leader of the conspiracy against the king unmasked in 1212. This was a rebellion whose leaders were known as 'the Northerners' yet whose solidarity derived from more southerly connections, not least to the Clare estates in Essex and East Anglia.

The charter itself, of which four 'original' single-sheet copies survive, is dated 15 June 1215. Peace was restored, with a mutual exchange of oaths and a great banquet a few days later. For a brief period, both the king and the charter's twenty-five barons sought to exercise executive authority in the English county courts. But no such settlement could endure. As a contemporary joked, no system could work that condemned John to become merely 'the twenty-fifth king in England'.[2] The barons refused to relinquish London. Archbishop Langton, in theory acting as a neutral arbiter, in reality far more sympathetic to the baronial than the royal cause, refused to surrender either the Tower of London or Rochester Castle: strongholds vital to England's defences against French invasion. The Pope, to whom a copy of the charter was despatched, immediately condemned it as the outcome of wicked conspiracy: an attempt to force oaths upon a king whose promises were sworn under compulsion and not by his own voluntary will.

The papal condemnation was issued on 24 August 1215. Already, long before it reached England, the king was again raising an army, summoning mercenaries to his aid. On 5 September, at Dover, John's clerical supporters threatened the barons and Archbishop Langton with a sentence of excommunication, imposed a week or so later. On the same day, 5 September, the king commanded that knights serve in his garrison at Winchester 'so long as war endures'. After less than eleven full weeks of the peace declared at Runnymede, war was officially resumed.

Yet Magna Carta's significance endured. A dead letter in the reign of King John, it was revived as a manifesto of good government, in the opening years of the reign of his son, Henry III. By such means it was to achieve astonishing fame, both in the thirteeth century and beyond. But nobody witnessing its failure in the summer of 1215 could possibly have anticipated its future apotheosis. The barons who went to war against John, from September 1215 until the king's death just over a year later, did so not in defence of Magna Carta or any political manifesto. Rather, they fought in fear for their lives, having no real choice between rebellion and potentially fatal surrender. Techniques that John had learned at his father's knee as long ago as the 1170s now came into play. Better, his father had taught him, to provoke your enemies and crush them than seek appeasement or allow conspiracies to fester.

John had overwhelming advantages. He had troops and, if not cash, then the ability to raise credit. He had papal support. His opponents were united only by their mistrust of the king. For the rest, they were as likely to fight among themselves as to make common cause. The baronial leaders feared venturing far from London, even when, from mid October to early December 1215, John laid siege to Rochester Castle, eventually capturing it after a campaign of more than eight weeks. The two months John spent at Rochester, indeed, represent the longest period he had spent in any one place since his earliest childhood. By 30 November, he was ready to press home his advantage. Commanding his constable at Dover to send 'by day and night forty of the fattest bacon pigs from those least worth eating, to be used to fetch fire beneath the [castle] keep', presumably to supply grease by which charges could be ignited and mines be sprung, he brought down the south-eastern tower of the castle.[3] The damage remains visible even today.

Having taken a rich haul of prisoners, John then moved north. He spent Christmas 1215 at Nottingham. From there he launched a devastating attack on the castles of Yorkshire and Northumbria. By 17 January 1216, he was at Haddington in East Lothian, only twenty miles from Edinburgh.

Meanwhile, rather than openly confront him, the barons in London sought aid from France. In October 1215, the first French troops had landed at the mouth of the River Orwell in Suffolk. In May 1216, Louis of France, King Philip's son and heir, crossed to Sandwich. As the husband of Blanche of Castile, herself a granddaughter of Henry II of England, Louis claimed the throne of England. In so doing, he denounced John as a tyrant and murderer lawfully deposed both by his barons and by his overlord, the King of France. At Sandwich, John was once again presented with an opportunity for a decisive battle. He is said to have observed the French landing, perhaps from Barham Down. Once again, his nerve failed him. As at Nottingham in 1194, Rouen in 1203, Angers in 1206 and La Roche in 1214, having sought battle, he then declined it. Battle avoidance was yet another lesson learned from his father and his heroic elder brother. This too was to cost John dear.

Four months of pillage ensued, with atrocities committed

both by barons and royalists. Southern England was laid waste. The French occupied London, took Winchester, and besieged both Windsor and Dover. John fought back from the West Country, with Corfe as his chief centre of operations. In September, he struck eastwards via Oxford to East Anglia and Lincolnshire. On Tuesday 11 October, he attempted to cross the estuarial quicksands of the Wash, from King's Lynn in the direction of Spalding.

Hunting and falconry had long been John's delight. Even on campaign in France in 1214, he had been accompanied by his huntsmen, hounds and hawks. Falconry for herons and cranes was a sport best pursued in autumn along the marshes and river banks where such prey abounded. Was it for this reason that John veered away from the main road from King's Lynn into Lincolnshire and instead struck out, across dykes and marshland? Whatever his motive, the outcome was chaos.

John became separated from his baggage train, itself cut off by the tide and eventually swallowed in the Fenland mud. What precisely was lost remains disputed. The crown jewels? Barrel-loads of silver? The robes and relics of the king's chapel, or perhaps merely the pack horses? If and when archaeology comes to the rescue, we may have answers. Meanwhile, the chroniclers almost certainly exaggerate the losses, portraying John as another Pharoah, his army engulfed in the waters of a revenging sea. What is clear is that John's crossing of the Wash was yet another humiliation. By the time he reached Swineshead on the Lincolnshire side of the estuary, he was exhausted and no doubt furious.

This was a king who had lived in the saddle all his life. As with his father before him, such frenetic movement, across England, Ireland and France, had taken its toll. A French chronicler reports the king, at the time of the Runnymede negotiations, immobilized by pains in his legs. Rather than acknowledge subjection, by themselves going to greet the king, the barons had insisted that John be carried into their presence on a litter. Even then they had remained seated, refusing the customary courtesy owed to kings.[4] From Swineshead, John struggled on to Newark, on the River Trent. There he died, a week after his crossing of the Wash, on the night of Tuesday 18 / Wednesday 19 October 1216. He was forty-nine years old.

Much later it was to be claimed that he was killed by poison, administered in a dish of pears: revenge for his attempted seduction of the Abbot of Swineshead's sister. In reality, the cause of death was almost certainly dysentery, according to one chronicler brought on by a meal of peaches and new cider.[5] As contemporaries might have noticed, John's losses in the Wash and his death both occurred on Tuesdays, Becket's holy day: the same day of the week, coincidentally, on which both Geoffrey and Richard, John's elder brothers, had died. Like his father before him, John suffered the ultimate indignity, robbed on his deathbed by members of his own household, his corpse plundered of all decent covering.

John's death was unexpected. No proper arrangements had been made either for his burial or for the accession of his son Henry. At Sleaford, on the road to Newark, on or around 15 October, a dossier of letters had been hurriedly drafted, appointing executors, promising gifts to religion and to discharge the king's crusading vows, and placing the future Henry III under papal protection. After death, John's body was disembowelled, as was customary. With his intestines set aside for burial at nearby Croxton Abbey, his eviscerated corpse was carried across country to Worcester. A few months earlier, John himself had threatened to put Worcester to the torch. There is no evidence that he was particularly devoted to either the city or its cathedral church. Probably he had hoped for burial either with his father, mother and brother, at Fontevraud on the Loire, or at his own Cistercian foundation at Beaulieu. In the circumstances of 1216, with both Fontevraud and Beaulieu in French hands, Worcester, scene of the king's last peacetime Christmas, was chosen simply as a place of safety, as far as possible from the ragings of civil war.

William Marshal, the man who seventeen years earlier had helped raise John to the throne, now led the cortège that conducted him to his final resting place. William later reclaimed the costs of two silk cloths he supplied to cover John's catafalque.[6] John's tomb and effigy at Worcester as they now survive were not completed until the 1230s. The Purbeck marble effigy is unique in showing John flanked by the saints, with his naked sword thrust into the mouth of a lion trampled beneath his feet. The intention perhaps was to invoke Psalm 91, claiming protection for a just ruler who will 'trample' the 'lion and the dragon'. The reality was that John, mocked in his lifetime as 'Softsword', was generally assumed to be burning in the flames of Hell. Even the sword displayed in the lion's mouth at Worcester is bent or twisted at its tip: a 'soft sword' indeed! Walter of

Guisborough, writing in the fourteenth century, tells us of a priest sympathetic to John, who prayed for the late king's soul. In a dream, the priest was instructed to turn to the Bible, but to Psalm 52 rather than Psalm 91.[7] Psalm 52 curses all wicked rulers, condemned to mockery and God's vengeance. The priest, so we are told, took the hint and ceased his prayers.

John died as he had reigned, a failure. At the time of his death, Magna Carta had little significance save as a symbol of peace betrayed. England was engulfed in civil war, with the Scots ravaging the north, the Welsh in the west, and a French prince ruling from London. To John's contemporaries, the real failure of his reign lay as much in France as in England, in the loss of Normandy and Anjou, in the crimes from which that loss emerged, and in John's subsequent inability to reconquer his ancestral lands, even at the cost of excommunication, interdict and the surrender of his sovereignty to Pope Innocent. John's surrender to the Pope and his charter granting freedom of election to the Church were preserved into the reign of his successor with far greater solemnity than the charter issued at Runnymede.

Of the Runnymede charter four iconic originals survive today. But until the nineteenth century none of them was copied into any official government record. Instead they gathered dust in one or other of the locations, for the most part cathedral churches, to which the detritus of the failed peace of 1215 had been consigned. Magna Carta as received in English law was not the charter of Runnymede but the revised and much altered charter issued by Henry III a decade later.

On the positive side – if positive is the right word – John can be credited with introducing English law and administration into Ireland. He thereby cemented relations between colony and colonizer that were to have a uniquely troubled posterity over the next eight hundred years. After John's two visits, no English sovereign was to enter Ireland until Richard II in the 1390s, and thereafter the equally ill-omened Oliver Cromwell. The skills John first learned in Ireland served him poorly in his dealings with either France or England. Where there had been peace, he brought conflict. Where there had been a degree of harmony between king and barons, he sowed mistrust and eventually rebellion. This was perhaps not an evil king, nor even the pantomine villain of later legend. John lacked neither brains nor guile. But his political intelligence, like his personality, was warped by cruelty, dishonesty and mistrust.

One of the king's grandsons, born in 1232, was named in his honour but failed to survive infancy. In more recent times, the only royal prince christened John, the youngest son of George V, died in 1919 aged only thirteen, an epileptic, hidden away by his parents. Long before this, in the 1370s, when the barons of Richard II threatened to make common cause with the king's uncle, John of Gaunt, it was widely murmured that there should be no more talk of kings in England named John. Since then, there has been no such talk. And there probably never will be.

Notes

INTRODUCTION

1. Sidney Painter, *The Reign of King John* (Baltimore: Johns Hopkins University Press, 1949), p. vii, and cf. Stephen Church, *King John and the Road to Magna Carta* (New York: Basic Books, 2015), first published as *King John: England, Magna Carta and the Making of a Tyrant* (London: Macmillan, 2015), and Marc Morris, *King John: Treachery, Tyranny and the Road to Magna Carta* (London: Hutchinson, 2015).
2. Rudyard Kipling, 'The Reeds of Runnymede', 1922 (for the poem in full, see https://www.bartleby.com/364/398.html).
3. David Hume, *The History of England*, 6 vols (London: A. Millar, 1762), vol. 1, p. 395.
4. Walter Scott, *Ivanhoe* (Edinburgh: Archibald Constable and Co., 1820), vol. 1, p. 144 (ch. 8).
5. William Stubbs, *The Constitutional History of England*, 3 vols (Oxford: Clarendon Press, 1874–8), vol. 2, p. 17.
6. See Josiah Cox Russell, *Twelfth Century Studies* (New York: AMS Press, 1978), pp. 64–5, for the height of Henry II and of Richard I, citing Gerald of Wales.

1. CHILDHOOD, YOUTH AND EXILE

1. John 20:2.
2. Continuation of the chronicle of Richard of Poitiers, in *Recueil des historiens des Gaules et de la France*, ed. M. Bouquet et al., 24 vols (Paris: 1738–1904), vol. 12, pp. 419–21 ('King of the North'); Guillaume le Breton, *Philippidos*, Bk III, line 311, in *Oeuvres de Rigord et de Guillaume le Breton*, ed. H.-F. Delaborde, 2 vols (Paris: Librairie Renouard, 1882–5), vol. 2, p. 77 ('King of London').
3. Gerald of Wales, *De Principis Instructione/Instruction for a Ruler*, ed. and trans. R. Bartlett (Oxford: Oxford University Press, 2018), pp. 702–3.
4. English translation in Giraldus Cambrensis (Gerald of Wales), *Expugnatio Hibernica: The Conquest of Ireland*, ed. A. B. Scott and F. X. Martin (Dublin: Royal Irish Academy, 1978).
5. *Rotuli Curiae Regis: Rolls and Records of the Court Held before the King's Justiciars or Justices*, ed. F. Palgrave, 2 vols (London: Eyre, 1835), vol. 2, pp. 172–3.

2. A CATALOGUE OF INFAMY?

1. *Magna Vita Sancti Hugonis: The Life of St Hugh of Lincoln*, ed. D. L. Douie and D. H. Farmer, 2 vols (Oxford: Clarendon Press, 1985), vol. 2, p. 144.

2. Ibid., pp. 138–9.

3. For Isabella, including the vexed question of her age, see N. Vincent, 'Isabella of Angoulême: John's Jezebel', in *King John: New Interpretations*, ed. S. D. Church (Woodbridge: Boydell & Brewer, 1999), pp. 165–219.

4. *The History of William Marshal*, ed. A. J. Holden, S. Gregory and D. Crouch, 3 vols (London: Anglo-Norman Text Society, 2002–6), vol. 2, pp. 162–3, line 13237; vol. 3, p. 150n., here accepting the editors' correction to the words as copied, 'uis de cité', which might be translated as 'you city gate' or 'you stay-at-home'.

5. *The Historical Works of Gervase of Canterbury*, ed. W. Stubbs, 2 vols (London: Longman, 1879–80), vol. 2, pp. 92–3.

6. *Rotuli Litterarum Clausarum in Turri Londinensi Asservati*, ed. T. D. Hardy, 2 vols (London: Record Commission, 1833–44), vol. 1, p. 2 (23 June 1204).

3. FROM THE FRYING PAN
INTO THE FIRE

1. P. D. A. Harvey, 'The English Inflation of 1180–1220', *Past and Present*, vol. 61 (1973), pp. 3–30.

2. *History of William Marshal*, ed. Holden et al., vol. 2, pp. 158–9, lines 13171–4.

3. Matthew Paris, *Historia Anglorum*, ed. F. Madden, 3 vols (London: Longman, 1866–9), vol. 2, p. 104.

4. *Rotuli Litterarum Patentium in Turri Londinensi Asservati*, ed. T. D. Hardy (London: Record Commission, 1835), p. 72.

5. The king's letters, circa September 1210, setting out his version of Braose's disgrace, are translated by David Crouch in *Magna Carta and the England of King John*, ed. J. S. Loengard (Woodbridge: Boydell & Brewer, 2010), pp. 168–80.

6. *Histoire des ducs de Normandie et des rois d'Angleterre*, ed. F. Michel (Paris: Société de l'Histoire de France, 1840), pp. 114–15.

7. N. Barratt, 'The Revenue of King John', *English Historical Review*, vol. 111 (1996), pp. 835–55.

8. 'Annales S. Edmundi', in *Ungedruckte Anglo-Normannische Gechichtsquellen*, ed. F. Liebermann (Strasbourg: 1879), pp. 153–4.

9. *Select Pleas of the Crown*, vol. 1: *AD 1200–1225*, ed. F. W. Maitland, Selden Society 1 (1888), pp. 67–75, no. 115.

10. Roger of Wendover, in Matthew Paris, *Chronica Majora*, ed. H. R. Luard, 7 vols (London: Longman, 1872–83), vol. 2, p. 550.

11. *Foedera*, ed. T. Rymer, rev. A. Clarke and F. Holbrooke, 4 vols in 7 parts (London: 1816–39), vol. 1, part 1 (1066–1272), p. 114.

4. THE WORST OF ALL OUR KINGS

1. Matthew Paris, *Chronica Majora*, ed. Luard, vol. 2, p. 668.

2. *Histoire des ducs de Normandie*, ed. Michel, p. 105.

3. *Oeuvres de Rigord et de Guillaume le Breton*, ed. Delaborde, vol. 2, p. 174.

4. *The Historical Collections of Walter of Coventry*, ed. W. Stubbs, 2 vols (London: Longman, 1872–3), vol. 2, p. 232, whence J. C. Holt, *The Northerners: A Study in the Reign of King John* (Oxford: Clarendon Press, 1961), p. 143.

5. *History of William Marshal*, ed. Holden et al., vol. 2, pp. 128–31, lines 12582–4.

6. Ibid., pp. 162–3, line 13237, and vol. 3, p. 150n.

7. *The Annals of Loch Cé*, ed. and trans. W. H. Hennessy, 2 vols (London: Longman, 1871), vol. 1, pp. 242–3.

8. *History of William Marshal*, ed. Holden et al., vol. 2, pp. 168–73, lines 13355–13419.

9. *Histoire des ducs de Normandie*, ed. Michel, pp. 105–6.

10. Ibid., pp. 104–5.

11. The 'Romance of Fulk fitz Warin', translated in *Medieval Outlaws: Ten Tales in Modern English*, ed. T. H. Ohlgren (Stroud: Sutton, 1998).

12. Roger of Wendover and Matthew Paris, in Matthew Paris, *Chronica Majora*, ed. Luard, vol. 2, pp. 481–2, 563.

13. S. Painter, 'Norwich's Three Geoffreys', *Speculum*, vol. 28 (1953), pp. 808–13.

14. *Rotuli Litterarum Patentium*, ed. Hardy, pp. 137b, 199; *Rotuli Litterarum Clausarum*, ed. Hardy, vol. 1, p. 330.

15. For the clearest attempt to whitewash King John, see D. M. Stenton, *English Justice Between the Norman Conquest and the Great Charter, 1066–1215* (Philadelphia: American Philosophical Society, 1964), with earlier commentary by C. W. Hollister, 'King John and the Historians', *Journal of British Studies*, vol. 1 (1961), pp. 1–19.

16. *Rotuli Litterarum Patentium*, ed. Hardy, p. 17b.

17. Matthew Paris, *Chronica Majora*, ed. Luard, vol. 2, p. 534.

18. *Documents Illustrative of English History in the Thirteenth and Fourteenth Centuries*, ed. H. Cole (London: Record Commission, 1844), p. 234.

19. N. Vincent, *Peter des Roches: An Alien in English Politics, 1205–1238* (Cambridge: Cambridge University Press, 1996), p. 70, citing Pipe Roll Society, New Series 24 (1951), p. 172.

20. *Rotuli de Oblatis et Finibus in Turri Londinensi Asservati, Tempore Regis Johannis*, ed. T. D. Hardy (London: Record Commission, 1835), p. 275.

21. *Rotuli Litterarum Clausarum*, ed. Hardy, vol. 1, p. 175b.

22. Ibid., p. 192.

23. *Documents Illustrative of English History*, ed. Cole, p. 250.

24. See *Rotuli Litterarum Clausarum*, ed. Hardy, vol. 1, p. 281b, with images and commentary at: http://magnacarta.cmp.uea.ac.uk/read/feature_of_the_month/Mar_2015_3

25. For this, as for the Robin Hood legends more generally, see J. C. Holt, *Robin Hood*, 2nd edn (London: Thames & Hudson, 1982).

26. Guillaume le Breton, in *Oeuvres de Rigord et de Guillaume le Breton*, ed. Delaborde, vol. 1, p. 311.

27. *The Chronicle of Walter of Guisborough*, ed. H. Rothwell, Camden Society (London: 1957), pp. 152–3.

28. M. Lovatt, 'Archbishop Geoffrey of York: A Problem in Anglo-French Maternity', in *Records, Administration and Aristocratic Society in the Anglo-Norman Realm*, ed. N. Vincent (Woodbridge: Boydell Press, 2009), pp. 91–123.

29. *Magna Vita Sancti Hugonis*, ed. Douie and Farmer, vol. 2, p. 138; *Rotuli de Liberate ac de Misis et Praestitis, Regnante Johanne*, ed. T. D. Hardy (London: Record Commission, 1844), p. 23.

30. Matthew Paris, *Chronica Majora*, ed. Luard, vol. 3, p. 222.

31. *Rotuli Litterarum Patentium*, ed. Hardy, p. 145.

32. Ibid., p. 77b.

33. *Rotuli Litterarum Clausarum*, ed. Hardy, vol. 1, p. 108.

34. Ibid., p. 203, and for the French letter of January 1215, see: http://magnacarta. cmp.uea.ac.uk/read/feature_of_the_month/Jan_2015

35. *Histoire de ducs de Normandie*, ed. Michel, pp. 150–51.

36. Holt, *The Northerners*, p. 34.

37. Roger of Wendover, in Matthew Paris, *Chronica Majora*, ed. Luard, vol. 2, pp. 532–3.

38. Vincent, *Peter des Roches*, pp. 73–4; idem, 'Hugh de Neville and his Prisoners', *Archives*, vol. 20 (1992), pp. 190–97.

39. *Historical Works of Gervase of Canterbury*, ed. Stubbs, vol. 2, p. lix.

40. J. R. Maddicott, 'The Oath of Marlborough, 1209: Fear, Government and Popular Allegiance in the Reign of King John', *English Historical Review*, vol. 126 (2011), pp. 281–318.

41. H. G. Richardson and G. O. Sayles, *The Irish Parliament in the Middle Ages*, 2nd edn (Philadelphia: University of Pennsylvania Press, 1964), pp. 286–7.

42. *Foedera*, ed. Rymer, p. 112; *Rotuli Litterarum Patentium*, ed. Hardy, p. 114b.

43. *Select Pleas of the Crown*, ed. Maitland, pp. 67–75, no. 115.

5. THE RECKONING AT RUNNYMEDE

1. J. C. Holt, *The Northerners*, 2nd edn (Oxford: Clarendon Press, 1992), p. xv.

2. Matthew Paris, *Chronica Majora*, ed. Luard, vol. 2, p. 611.

3. *Rotuli Litterarum Clausarum*, ed. Hardy, vol. 1, p. 238b.

4. *Histoire des ducs de Normandie*, ed. Michel, p. 151.

5. Roger of Wendover, in Matthew Paris, *Chronica Majora*, ed. Luard, vol. 2, pp. 667–8.

6. *Roll of Divers Accounts for the Early Years of the Reign of Henry III*, ed. F. A. Cazel (London: Pipe Roll Society, 1982), p. 36.

7. *Chronicle of Walter of Guisborough*, ed. Rothwell, p. 156, allowing here for the fact that the Catholic Vulgate Psalms 51 and 90 are Psalms 52 and 91 as presented in the Protestant Bible.

Further Reading

Among the many modern biographers, the classic study by Sidney Painter, *The Reign of King John* (Baltimore: Johns Hopkins University Press, 1949), contains a wealth of detail but without the narrative framework supplied subsequently by W. L. Warren, *King John* (London: Eyre & Spottiswoode, 1961), and Stephen Church, *King John: England, Magna Carta and the Making of a Tyrant* (London: Macmillan, 2015). Alternative viewpoints can be found in the lives by Ralph V. Turner, *King John* (London: Longman, 1994), Marc Morris, *King John: Treachery, Tyranny and the Road to Magna Carta* (London: Hutchinson, 2015), and (still sprightly more than a century after its first publication) Kate Norgate, *John Lackland* (London: Macmillan, 1902). On the politics of John's reign, there is the incomparable study by J. C. Holt, *The Northerners: A Study in the Reign of King John* (Oxford: Clarendon Press, 1961; 2nd edn, 1992), David Carpenter, *Magna Carta* (London: Penguin, 2015), and the collection of themed essays edited by Stephen Church as *King John: New Interpretations* (Woodbridge: Boydell & Brewer, 1999). For Magna Carta and its background, besides Carpenter, see Nicholas Vincent, *Magna Carta: Origins and Legacy* (Oxford: Bodleian Library Publishing, 2015), and *Magna Carta: A Very Short Introduction* (Oxford: Oxford University Press, 2012). It is a pity that many of the primary sources for John's reign remain untranslated. For exceptions here, see the translation by John Allen Giles (long out of print) of *Roger of Wendover's Flowers of History*, 2 vols (London: H. G. Bohn, 1849), and the vivid modern edition of *The History of William Marshal*, edited by A. J. Holden, S. Gregory and D. Crouch, 3 vols (London: Anglo-Norman Text Society, 2002–6), with a more easily accessible

English version by Nigel Bryant (Woodbridge: Boydell & Brewer, 2016). Although the vast bulk of the administrative records of the reign can be accessed only in Latin editions, published for the most part under the editorship of Thomas Duffus Hardy before 1850, there are many snippets and new discoveries to be explored online at the Magna Carta Project website (http://magnacarta.cmp.uea.ac.uk).

Picture Credits

1. John, Henry II, Richard I and Henry III depicted by Matthew Paris *c.*1240 (© British Library Board. All Rights Reserved/Bridgeman Images)
2. John's hunting portrait (© British Library Board. All Rights Reserved/Bridgeman Images)
3. John's great seal (reproduced by permission of the Provost and Fellows of Eton College)
4. Angers on the Loire (Heritage Image Partnership Ltd/Alamy Stock Photo)
5. Dublin Castle (Saiko3p/iStock)
6. Queen Isabella, John's second wife (DEA/S. VANNINI/Getty Images)
7. The seal of Arthur, Duke of Brittany (© Centre Historique des Archives Nationales, Paris, France/Bridgeman Images)
8. Corfe Castle (David Noton Photography/Alamy Stock Photo)
9. The seal of Stephen Langton, Archbishop of Canterbury (reproduced courtesy of the Chapter of Canterbury Cathedral)
10. The *Chronica Majora* by Matthew Paris (© Bridgeman Images)
11. Carrickfergus Castle (Krzysztof Nahlik/Alamy Stock Photo)
12. Runnymede, with Windsor Castle in the distance (© National Trust)
13. The Articles of the Barons (© British Library Board. All Rights Reserved/Bridgeman Images)
14. Magna Carta (World History Archive/Alamy Stock Photo)
15. John's tomb at Worcester Cathedral (photograph by Mr Christopher Guy, Worcester Cathedral Archaeologist. Reproduced by permission of the Chapter of Worcester Cathedral (UK))

Acknowledgements

Having written perhaps too many books on Magna Carta, a couple of them in the charter's eight-hundredth anniversary year, 2015, I vowed never to write another. The current essay is therefore a study of King John from which Magna Carta is chiefly conspicuous by its absence. Rather than *Hamlet* without the Dane, what I hope I have presented here is *Hamlet* without a great deal of teleological Danish constitutionalism. As ever, I am indebted to the advice of friends and colleagues, most notably Sophie Ambler, Martin Aurell, the late John Baldwin, Paul Brand, Claire Breay, David Carpenter, Stephen Church, Hugh Doherty, Seán Duffy, Marie Therese Flanagan, John Gillingham, the late Sir James Holt, Kate Parker, Tom Penn, Daniel Power, Henry Summerson and Louise Wilkinson. My first encounter with John occurred more than fifty years ago, in the poetry of A. A. Milne, then in the Ladybird book so evocatively illustrated by John Kenney. Later, Henry Mayr-Harting and John Maddicott introduced me to the academic debates, from Stubbs onwards. It was at their recommendation that I first picked up Jim Holt's *Northerners*, still a sensationally good read: one of the best books of medieval history ever written. All future studies of John will be judged by comparison with Holt's portrait. I do not claim to have replaced that portrait. I have, however, retouched it, lending various of its Yorkshire draperies a rather jauntier Franco-Hibernian slant.

Index

Penguin Monarchs

THE HOUSES OF WESSEX AND DENMARK

Athelstan*	Tom Holland
Aethelred the Unready	Richard Abels
Cnut	Ryan Lavelle
Edward the Confessor	David Woodman

THE HOUSES OF NORMANDY, BLOIS AND ANJOU

William I*	Marc Morris
William II	John Gillingham
Henry I	Edmund King
Stephen	Carl Watkins
Henry II*	Richard Barber
Richard I	Thomas Asbridge
John	Nicholas Vincent

THE HOUSE OF PLANTAGENET

Henry III	Stephen Church
Edward I*	Andy King
Edward II	Christopher Given-Wilson
Edward III*	Jonathan Sumption
Richard II*	Laura Ashe

THE HOUSES OF LANCASTER AND YORK

Henry IV	Catherine Nall
Henry V*	Anne Curry
Henry VI	James Ross
Edward IV	A. J. Pollard
Edward V	Thomas Penn
Richard III	Rosemary Horrox

* Now in paperback

THE HOUSE OF TUDOR

Henry VII	Sean Cunningham
Henry VIII*	John Guy
Edward VI*	Stephen Alford
Mary I*	John Edwards
Elizabeth I	Helen Castor

THE HOUSE OF STUART

James I	Thomas Cogswell
Charles I*	Mark Kishlansky
[Cromwell*	David Horspool]
Charles II*	Clare Jackson
James II	David Womersley
William III & Mary II*	Jonathan Keates
Anne	Richard Hewlings

THE HOUSE OF HANOVER

George I	Tim Blanning
George II	Norman Davies
George III	Jeremy Black
George IV	Stella Tillyard
William IV	Roger Knight
Victoria*	Jane Ridley

THE HOUSES OF SAXE-COBURG & GOTHA AND WINDSOR

Edward VII*	Richard Davenport-Hines
George V*	David Cannadine
Edward VIII*	Piers Brendon
George VI*	Philip Ziegler
Elizabeth II*	Douglas Hurd

* Now in paperback